HATCHMENTS IN BRITAIN

9

Herefordshire, Shropshire, Wales and Scotland

HATCHMENTS IN BRITAIN

9

Herefordshire, Shropshire, Wales and Scotland

Edited by
PETER SUMMERS, F.S.A.
and
JOHN E. TITTERTON

PHILLIMORE

1994

Published by
PHILLIMORE & CO. LTD.
Shopwyke Manor Barn, Chichester, West Sussex

© Herefordshire, Shropshire, Wales—John E. Titterton
Scotland—C. J. Burnett
1994

ISBN 0 85033 912 X

Printed and bound in Great Britain by
HARTNOLLS LTD.,
Bodmin, Cornwall.

CONTENTS

General Introduction ix
Abbreviations xv
Herefordshire 1
Shropshire 21
Wales and Monmouthshire 69
Scotland 109
Index 129

ILLUSTRATIONS

HEREFORDSHIRE
Canon Frome 1: For Grace Anne Hopton, 1839 2

SHROPSHIRE
Great Ness 1: For John Edwards, 1850 22

WALES
Llanbedrog 2: For Lt-Gen. Sir Love Parry Jones-Parry,
    1853 70

SCOTLAND
Blair Athol 2: For James Robertson, 1803 110

GENERAL INTRODUCTION

Hatchments are a familiar sight to all those who visit our parish churches. They are not only decorative, but of great interest to the herald, genealogist and local historian. It is therefore surprising that—apart from local surveys in a few counties mostly in recent years—no attempt has yet been made to record them on a national scale. This series will, it is hoped, remedy the deficiency; it is proposed to publish separate volumes covering all English counties as well as Wales, Scotland and Ireland.

It is probable that no volume will be complete. Previously unrecorded hatchments will turn up from time to time; many have already been found in obscure places such as locked cupboards and ringing chambers. There are likely to be some inaccuracies, for hatchments are often hung high up in dark corners, and the colours may have faded or been darkened with age and grime. Identification is a problem if the arms do not appear anywhere in print: and even if the arms are identified, pedigrees of the family may not always be available. But enough has been done to make publication worthwhile; the margin to the pages will perhaps allow for pencilled amendments and notes.

Since I began the survey in 1952 many hatchments, probably evicted at the time of Victorian restorations, have been replaced in the churches from whence they came. On the other hand during the same period just as many hatchments have been destroyed. An excuse often made by incumbents is that they are too far gone to repair, or that the cost of restoration is too great. Neither reason is valid. If any incumbent, or anyone who has the responsibility for the care of hatchments which need attention, will write to me, I shall be happy to tell him how the hatchments may be simply and satisfactorily restored at a minimal cost. It is hoped that the publication of this survey will help to draw attention to the importance of these heraldic records.

The diamond-shaped hatchment, which originated in the Low Countries, is a debased form of the medieval achievement—the shield, helm, and other accoutrements carried at the funeral of a noble or knight. In this country it was customary for the hatchment to be hung outside the house during the period of mourning, and thereafter be placed in the church. This practice, begun in the early 17th century, is by no means entirely obsolete, for about 80 examples have so far been recroded for the present century.

Closely allied to the diamond hatchment, and contemporary with the earlier examples, are rectangular wooden panels bearing coats of arms. As some of these bear no inscriptions and a black/white or white/black background, and as some otherwise typical hatchments bear anything from initials and a date to a long inscription beginning 'Near here lies buries ...', it will be appreciated that it is not always easy to draw a line between the true hatchment and the memorial panel. Any transitional types will therefore also be listed, but armorial boards which are clearly intended as simple memorials will receive only a brief note.

With hatchments the background is of unique significance, making it possible to tell at a glance whether it is for a bachelor or spinster, husband or wife, widower or widow. These different forms all appear on the plate immediately following this introduction.

Royal Arms can easily be mistaken for hatchments, especially in the West Country where they are frequently of diamond shape and with a black background. But such examples often bear a date, which proves that they were not intended as hatchments. Royal hatchments, however, do exist; any examples known will be included.

All hatchments are in the parish church unless otherwise stated, but by no means are they all in churches; many are in secular buildings and these, if they have no links with the parish in which they are now found, are listed at the end of the text. All hatchments recorded since the survey began are listed, including those which are now missing.

As with the previous volumes, although I did much of the original work for it, aided by many friends, a great deal more has been done in recent years by my co-Editor, John Titterton; and he will be entirely responsible for the final volume *History and Development of the Funeral Hatchment*, a task involving much original research.

The illustrations overleaf are the work of the late Mr. G. A. Harrison and will provide a valuable 'key' for those unfamiliar with the complexity of hatchment backgrounds.

One last, but important note. Every copy sold of this book helps a child in the Third World; for I have irrevocably assigned all royalties on the entire series to a charity, The Ockenden Venture.

PETER SUMMERS
Paddocks, Reading Road, Wallingford

1. MARRIED MAN
2. MARRIED WOMAN
3. BACHELOR
4. WIDOW
5. WIDOWER
6. SPINSTER

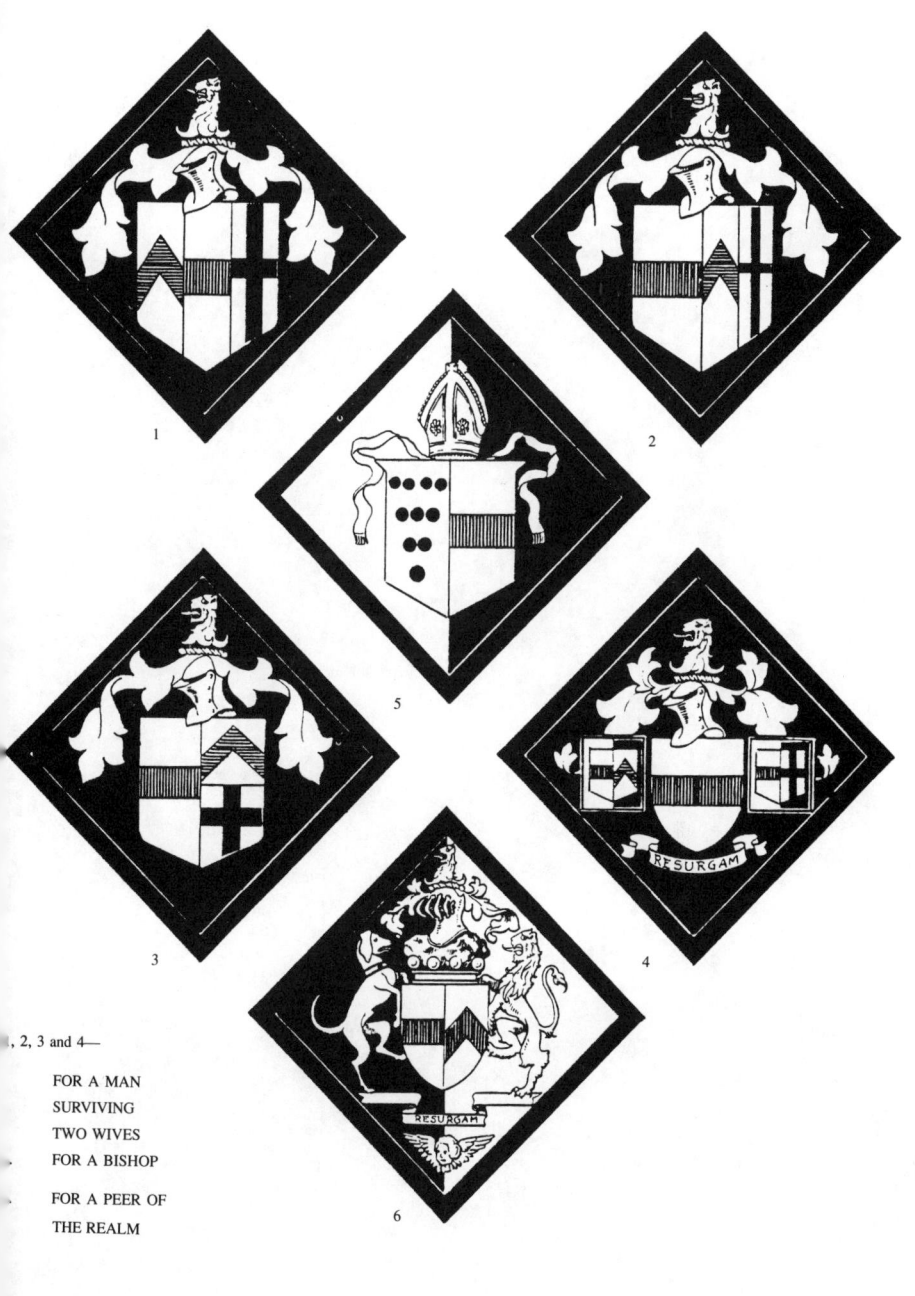

1, 2, 3 and 4—
FOR A MAN
SURVIVING
TWO WIVES
5. FOR A BISHOP
6. FOR A PEER OF
THE REALM

ABBREVIATIONS

B.P.	=	Burke's *Peerage, Baronetage and Knightage*
B.L.G.	=	Burke's *Landed Gentry*
B.E.P.	=	Burke's *Extinct and Dormant Peerages*
B.E.B.	=	Burke's *Extinct and Dormant Baronetcies*
V.C.H.	=	*Victoria County History*
D.N.B.	=	*Dictionary of National Biography*
M.I.	=	Monumental Inscription
P.R.	=	Parish Register
M.O.	=	*Musgrave's Obituary*
G.M.	=	*Gentleman's Magazine*
Gen. Mag	=	*Genealogists' Magazine*
M.G. & H.	=	*Miscellanea Genealogica et Heraldica*
Mormon	=	Mormon International Genealogical Index
G.E.C.	=	*The Complete Peerage*, G. E. Cockayne
G.E.C. Bt.	=	*The Complete Baronetage*, G. E. Cockayne
C.J.B.	=	C. J. Burnett, Ross Herald

NOTE

Blazons throughout are exactly as noted at the time of recording, not as they ought to be.

HEREFORDSHIRE

Canon Frome 1: For Grace Anne Hopton, 1839
(*Photograph by Mrs. C. M. Best*)

INTRODUCTION

There are 60 hatchments in this county. Some are of interest as hatchments alone, whilst others represent people with interesting backgrounds. The earliest hatchment in the county is also the earliest one so far identified in the country. It is at Eye and for John Blount who died in 1629. Although his wife survived him, the background is all black and it has a small inscription.

Another 17th-century hatchment is at Lower Brockhampton House (National Trust). It is for Thomas Habington of Hindlip Hall who was sentenced to death in 1606 for being involved with the gunpowder plot. He was reprieved but was confined to live within the county boundaries of Worcestershire and he died in 1647. The hatchment carried at his funeral is now at Spetchley Park, Worcestershire. So what was the purpose of this hatchment? The two are not identical.

Four more 17th-century hatchments are at Knill and form part of a series of nine to the Walsham family of Knill Court. However, these four may have been painted at a later date. All nine at Knill have an inscription or leather tag with the dates of death of both husband and wife. It would seem that all were painted to represent the death of the male partner with these tags added.

There are two other good family collections in the county: eight at Richards Castle to the Salway family and six at Tyberton to the Brydges family. At Holm Lacey there are four hatchments to the Scudamore family and their connections. One is for Charles, 11th Duke of Norfolk. He married two heiresses and has two escutcheons of pretence. His second wife was Frances, the Scudamore heiress, who was insane. The Duke had no heirs by either wife and his titles passed to a cousin. The Scudamore estates passed to the crown.

By curious coincidence two of the three hatchments at St Weonards have duplicates but are totally unrelated. The other hatchment for Charles Morgan is to be found at Lower Machen, Monmouth, and Anne Mynors-Baskerville has another hatchment at Winterbourne Bassett, Wiltshire. Her husband's hatchment is at Clyro, Wales.

These hatchments are recorded by several correspondents including the late Mr. W. Peplow who was also editor for Worcestershire. I am also very grateful to the Rev. F. M. Best who checked all of them.

JOHN E. TITTERTON
7 Cecil Aldin Drive, Tilehurst, Reading

ABBEY DORE

1. Dexter background black
Per pale azure and gules a chevron between three lions rampant or, a crescent gules for difference (Hoskyns), impaling, Per pale azure and gules a chevron between three lions rampant or (Hoskyns)
Crest: A lion's head erased and crowned or, from the mouth flames of fire or   Mantling: Gules and argent   Motto: Salus in Coelo
Unidentifield

2. Dexter background black
Qly, 1st and 4th, Per pale azure and gules a chevron between three lions rampant or (Hoskyns), 2nd and 3rd, Argent a chevron between three lions' heads erased azure, on a chief gules three cross crosslets or (Wren), impaling, Qly, 1st and 4th, Or ermined sable on a chevron gules between three roses gules barbed and seeded proper two swords argent hilted or (Ricketts), 2nd and 3rd, Barry of eight gules and or (Poyntz), over all a crescent sable for difference   Also, in pretence, over dexter coats, Wren
Crests: (on either side of a knight's helm)   Dexter, Out of a ducal coronet or, a lion's head erased, crowned or, from the mouth flames of fire proper   Sinister, A lion's head erased argent collared gules, charged on the neck with a cross crosslet gules and pierced through the neck with a broken spear proper headed argent embrued gules
Mantling: Gules and argent   Motto: Vincula da linguae vel tibi lingua dabit
The shield is borne on a Maltese cross; there is a similar but smaller cross suspended on a ribbon below the shield, above which is a scimitar fesswise point to the sinister argent hilted or
For Chandos Wren-Hoskyns, who m. 1837, Theodosia Ann Martha, dau. and heir of Christoper Roberts Wren, of Wroxhall Abbey, Co. Warwick, and 2nd, 1846, Anna Fane, youngest dau. of Charles Milner Ricketts, and d. 28 Nov. 1876.   (B.P. 1949 ed.)

BRAMPTON ABBOTS

1. All black background
Qly, 1st and 4th, Azure a cross between four caltraps or (Westfaling), 2nd, Or an anchor and cable sable (Chappell), 3rd, Or on a bend azure three Catherine wheels argent (Rudhall)
Crest: (no helm) A hand holding a spray of roses proper   No mantling
Motto: Mors janua vitæ   Palm branches flanking shield
Probably for Mrs. Mary Westfaling, d. 1830.   (Church guide)

BROCKHAMPTON Lower Brockhampton House
1. All black background
Qly of nine, 1st, Argent on a bend gules three eagles displayed or (Habington), 2nd, Gules a lion rampant double-queued argent (De Bosco), 3rd, Gules a fess and in chief two mullets argent (Poher), 4th, Sable five bezants in saltire and a chief or (Byfield), 5th, Sable a fess nebuly between six billets or (Domulton), 6th, Gules a fess between six fusils or, (Marescall), 7th, Gules a fess between six mascles or (Brockhampton), 8th, Gules three fusils in bend or (Marescall), 9th, Gules three lozenges or (Brockhampton), impaling, Qly, 1st, Argent a lion passant gules between on two bars sable three bezants (2,1) and in chief three stags heads cabossed sable (Parker), 2nd, Barry nebuly gules and or (Lovel), 3rd, Argent a lion rampant sable crowned or (Morley), 4th, Gules a bend fusilly or (Marshall)
Crest: An arm in armour embowed at the elbow proper   Mantling: Gules and argent
For Thomas Habington, of Hindlip, who m. Mary Parker, dau. of Edward, 12th Lord Morley, and d. 8 Oct. 1647.
(There is another hatchment (not identical) for Thomas Habington at Spetchley Park, Worcs)

CANON FROME
1. Sinister background black
Qly, 1st, Gules a lion rampant between eight crosses formy fitchy or (Hopton), 2nd, Argent on a chevron azure between three roses gules stalked and leaved vert three fleurs-de-lis or (Cope), 3rd, Gules two bars argent on each three mascles fessways sable, on a canton argent a leopard's face azure (Geere), 4th, Sable a chevron ermine between three trefoils slipped argent (   ), impaling, Argent a greyhound courant sable between three choughs, within a bordure engrailed gules charged with eight crosses formy or and as many bezants alternately (Williams)
Crest: Out of a ducal coronet or a griffin's head argent in the beak a bloody hand proper   No mantling   Motto: Resurgam
For Grace Anne, eldest dau. of John Williams, who m. 1807, the Rev. John Hopton, Vicar of Canon Frome, and d. 1 Oct. 1839.   (B.L.G. 5th ed.)

2. All black background
Williams arms only
Crest: A dexter arm embowed in armour the hand proper holding an oak branch vert fructed or   No mantling   Motto: Resurgam
Unidentified

DINMORE Chapel
1. All black background
Gules three crescents argent between seven cross crosslets fitchy or (Fleming)
Crest: A cubit arm in armour the hand proper grasping a dagger argent hilt and pommel or   Mantling: Gules and argent   Motto: In coelo quies
Unidentified

Herefordshire

EYE

1. All black background
Qly, 1st and 4th, Or three bars nebuly sable in chief a crescent gules (Blount), 2nd and 3rd, Or on a fess gules between three peacocks sable two lozenges fesswise in pale or (More), impaling, Gules a lion rampant reguardant or (Price)
Crest: A sun in splendour or charged with a foot in armour proper
Mantling: Gules and or   No motto
Inscribed around frame: These are the arms of Iohn Esquir and Elizabeth his wife he desceased the eleventh day of September in the yeare of our Lord 1629   A very small hatchment c. 2 ft x 2 ft
For John Blount, son of John Blount, of Eye, m. Elizabeth, dau. of James Price of Manachty, and d. 11 Sept. 1629. She d. 1632.   (Inscription on hatchment frame; Church guide;)

HOLME LACY

1. All black backgound
On a lozenge   Gules three stirrups leathered and buckled or (Scudamore), impaling, Sable a fleur-de-lis argent (Digby)
Viscountess's coronet   Motto: Scuto amoris divini
Supporters: Dexter, A horse sable, leathered and saddled or   Sinister, A bear sable ducally gorged or
For Frances, only dau. and heir of Simon, Lord Digby, who m. James, 3rd Viscount Sudamore (d. 2 Dec. 1716), and d. 3 May 1729.   (G.E.C.)

2. Sinister background black
Qly, 1st and 4th, qly i. & iv. France and England qly, ii. Scotland, iii. Ireland, over all a baton sinister compony azure and ermine (Fitzroy), 2nd and 3rd, Gules three stirrups leathered and buckled or (Scudamore)   In pretence: Scudamore
Motto: In coelo quies   Cherub's head above
For Frances, only dau. and heir of James, 3rd Viscount Scudamore, who m. Charles Fitzroy Scudamore, and d. 16 Feb. 1750.   (G.E.C.)

3. Dexter background black
Qly, 1st, Gules on a bend between six cross crosslets fitchy argent the Augmentation of Flodden (Howard), 2nd, Gules three lions passant guardant in pale or a label of three points argent (Brotherton), 3rd, Chequy or and azure (Warren), 4th, Gules a lion rampant argent (Mowbray)   Two escutcheons of pretence: Dexter, Azure a bull's head cabossed between three estoiles of six points argent (Copinger)   Sinister, Gules three stirrups leathered and buckled or (Scudamore)   Behind the shield in saltire two gold batons, ends sable (Earl Marshal)

Duke's coronet   Crest: On a chapeau gules and ermine a lion statant guardant tail extended or ducally gorged argent   Motto: Sola virtus invicta   Supporters: Dexter, a lion argent   Sinister, A horse argent holding in its mouth a slip of oak fructed proper
For Charles, 11th Duke of Norfolk, who m. 1st, 1767, Marian, only dau. and heir of John Coppinger, of Ballyvolane, co. Cork, and 2nd, 1771, Frances, dau. and heir of Charles Fitzroy Scudamore, and d. 16 Dec. 1815.   (G.E.C.)
(There is another hatchment for the 11th Duke of Norfolk, Sussex)

4. All black background
On a lozenge   Howard impaling Scudamore
Duchess's coronet   Motto and supporters: As 3.
For Frances, widow of Charles, 11th Duke of Norfolk at Arundel. She d. 22 Oct. 1820.   (G.E.C.)

KINSHAM

1. All black background
Azure a griffin passant and a chief or (Evelyn), impaling, Argent two bendlets between two martlets sable (Bradshaw)
Crest: A griffin passant or ducally gorged sable   Mantling: Gules and Argent   Motto: Resurgam
Unidentified

KNILL

1. All black background
Sable on a cross voided five crosses formy fitchy or (Walsham)   In pretence: Gules crusilly fitchy a lion rampant or (Knill)
Crest: A Saracen's head affronté proper wreathed at the temples argent and azure   Mantling: Sable and or   Motto: Dieu le veut
Inscribed over frame: A.D. 1639-1617, but hatchment does not appear to be as old as this; probably a copy
For John Walsham, of Presteigne, who m. Barbara, dau. and heiress of Francis Knill, of Knill Court, and d. 1639. She d. 1617.   (B.P. 1949 ed.; inscr. above hatchment)

2. All black background
Walsham, impaling, Gules three roundels argent each charged with a king in his robes bearing in his right hand a covered cup and in his left hand a sword all proper (Lyde)
Crest, mantling and motto: As 1.
Inscribed on leather tag above: 1648-1656, but definitely painted at a later date.
Despite background probably intended to be for John Walsham, of Knill Court, who m. Margaret, dau. of Roger Lyde, and d. 1648. She d. 1656. (Sources, as 1.)

Herefordshire

3. All grey background
Walsham, impaling, Vert a chevron between three wolves' heads erased or (Jones)
Crest, mantling and motto: As 1.
Inscribed above frame: 1677-1680, but hatchment not as old as this
For John Walsham of Knill Court, who m. Joanna, dau. of John Jones, of Llandetty Court, Brecon, and d. 1677. (Burke gives 1667). She d. 1680. (Sources, as 1.)

4. All black background
Walsham, impaling, to dexter, Gules two lions passant guardant argent (Lygon), and to sinister, Gules a chevron ermine between three eagles displayed argent (Childe)
Crest: As 1.   Mantling: Gules and argent   Skull in base
Inscribed on leather tag fixed to top of hatchment: 1674 1695 1685
For John Walsham, of Knill Court, who m. 1st, Elizabeth (d. 1674), dau. of Sir William Lygon, and 2nd, Elizabeth, dau. of Sir William Childe, of Kinlet, and d. 1695. She d. 1685.   (Sources, as 1.)

5. All black background
Walsham, impaling, Argent three bulls' heads cabossed sable (Morgan)
Crest: As 1.   Mantling: Gules and argent   Motto: Mors Lucrum mihi
Inscribed above hatchment: A.D. 1734-1713
For John Walsham, of Knill Court, who m. Hester, elder dau. and eventual co-heiress of Sir John Morgan, Bt., of Kinnersley Castle, and d. 1734. She d. 1713.   (Sources, as 1.)

6. All grey background
Walsham, impaling, Argent a fess between three lions rampant gules (Ford ?)
Crest: As 1.   Mantling: Gules and argent   No motto
Inscribed above hatchment: 1751-1792
Probably, despite background, for John Walsham, of Knill Court, who m. Elizabeth, dau. and co-heiress of Alderman Ford, of Hereford, and d. 1751. The arms do not appear for Ford in Burke's General Armory, but date would imply that this ascription is correct.   (Sources, as 1.)

7. All black background
Gules a griffin segreant holding a tilting spear or bearing a banner, argent a double-headed eagle sable (Garbett)   In pretence: Walsham
Crest: A double-headed eagle displayed sable   Mantling: Gules and argent
Inscribed above hatchment: 1801-1779
For Francis Garbett, of Huntingdon Park, Herefordshire, who m. 1767, Elizabeth, only child and heir of John Walsham, of Knill, and d. 1801. She d. 1779.   (Sources, as 1.)

8. Dexter background black

Qly, 1st, Walsham, 2nd, Per pale azure and gules a griffin segreant or holding a tilting spear with a banner, argent a cross azure (Garbett), 3rd, Gules crusilly fitchy a lion rampant or (Knill), 4th, Argent three bulls' heads cabossed sable (Morgan), impaling, Qly 1st and 4th, Argent a double-headed eagle displayed sable, 2nd and 3rd, Argent three firebrands inflamed gules; over all on an escutcheon argent a leg couped at the thigh sable (Hughes)
Crest: A demi-double-headed eagle displayed sable each wing charged with a cross formy fitchy between two swords or, round its neck an escutcheon argent charged with a Saracen's head proper   Mantling: Gules and argent   Motto: Resurgam   Skull in base
Inscribed above hatchment: A.D. 1819-1863
For John Garbett Walsham, of Knill Court, who m. 1804, Anna Maria, dau. and sole heiress of Hugh Hughes, and d. 1819. She d. 1863. (Sources, as 1.)

9. All black background

Qly, 1st and 4th, Walsham, 2nd and 3rd, Knill; over all on an escutcheon argent a leg couped at the thigh sable; in centre chief the Badge of Ulster, impaling, Sable a fess ermine between three bells argent (Bell)
Crest: As 8., but from a ducal coronet or, with scroll above inscribed, A fynno duw derfid   Motto: (below shield) Sub libertate quietem
Inscribed above hatchment: A.D. 1874-1857
For Sir John James Walsham, 1st Bt., who m. 1826, Sarah Frances, 2nd dau. of Matthew Bell, of Woolsington House, Northumberland, and d. 10 Aug. 1874. She d. 19 Aug. 1857.   (Sources, as 1.)

LEOMINSTER Museum

1. Dexter background black

Qly, 1st and 4th, Per fess argent and azure between a fess embattled counter-embattled counterchanged three fleurs-de-lis or (Wall), 2nd and 3rd, Argent a bend engrailed azure a canton gules, (   ), impaling, Gules a lion rampant within a bordure engrailed argent (   )
Crest: Out of a mural crown a wolf's head proper langued and collared embattled counter-embattled gules   Mantling: Or   Motto: Resurgam   Skull in base
Unidentified

MUCH MARCLE

1. All black background

Qly, 1st and 4th, Chequy gules and argent on a chief sable three eagles displayed or (Money), 2nd and 3rd, Vert a chevron between three fleurs-de-lis or (Kyrle), over all the Badge of Ulster
No crest   Mantling: Gules and argent   Motto: Nil moror ictus
Skull in base
For Major-Gen. Sir James Money-Kyrle, Bt. (cr. 1838), who m. 1811, Ann

Herefordshire 11

Caroline, dau. of Robert Taylor, of London, and d.s.p. 26 June 1843.
(B.L.G. 1937 ed.)

2. All black background

Qly of six, 1st, qly i. & iv. Kyrle, ii. & iii. Money, 2nd, Money, 3rd, Argent on a fess between six martlets gules three quartrefoils argent (Washbourne), 4th, Argent on a bend sable three eagles displayed or (Ernie), 5th, Kyrle, 6th, Azure a cross engrailed ermine (Stoughton), impaling, Qly, 1st and 4th, Gules a stag's head cabossed argent (Down), 2nd and 3rd, Per pale sable and gules a lion passant guardant argent (Neale)
Crest: Dexter, On a mount vert a hedgehog or   Sinister, An eagle's head erased per fess sable and argent collared gemel or in the mouth a fleur-de-lis or   Mantling: Gules and argent   Motto: In coelo quies
For the Rev. William Money-Kyrle, who m. 1805, Emma, dau. of Richard Down, of Halliwick Manor House, Middlesex, and d. 18 Jan. 1848.
(B.L.G. 1937 ed.)

3. Dexter background black

Azure a shakefork or ermined sable between three boars' heads erased close or langued gules (Shetliffe)   In pretence: Qly, 1st and 4th, Kyrle, 2nd and 3rd, Money
Crest: In front of a sun in splendour or a lion passant sable armed and langued gules   Mantling: Azure and or   Motto: A posse ad esse
For the Rev. George Thomas Shetliffe, 4th son of Joseph Shetliffe, of Goolwa, S. Australia, who m. 1934, Elizabeth Mary, only dau. and heir of the Ven. Rowland Tracy Ashe Money-Kyrle, and d. 5 Sept. 1956, aged 67.
(B.L.G. 1937 ed.; M.I. in churchyard)

RICHARDS CASTLE

1. Dexter background black

Qly, 1st, Sable a saltire engrailed or (Salwey), 2nd, Argent on a fess between six martlets gules three quartrefoils argent (Washbourne), 3rd, Gules a lion rampant argent crowned or (Musard), 4th, Or on a saltire engrailed sable a bezant (Trumym), impaling, Qly, 1st and 4th, Argent a bend engrailed sable (Radcliffe), 2nd and 3rd, Argent two bars gules on a canton gules a cinquefoil argent (Derwentwater)   To dexter of main shield, Salwey, impaling, Gules a fess vair between three molets argent (Baugh)   To sinister of main shield, Salwey, impaling, Radcliffe
Crest: A Saracen's head affronté couped at the shoulders proper, the right shoulder vested argent, the other bare, wreathed at the temples or and sable   Mantling: Gules and argent
For John Salwey, of Moor Park, who m. 1st, 1768, Anne, only dau. of Thomas Foliot Baugh, of Stonehouse, and 2nd,   Radcliffe, and d.
(B.L.G. 1937 ed.)

2. Sinister background black
Salwey In pretence: Ermine on a fess sable a castle triple-towered argent (Hill)
Motto: In caelo quies
Frame covered in black cloth
For Anna Maria, younger dau. and co-heir of Thomas Hill, of Court of Hill, Salop, who m. 1787, Theophilus Richard Salwey, of the Lodge, Ludlow, and d. 13 Aug. 1812.   (B.L.G. 1937 ed.)

3. All black background
Arms: As 2.
Crest and mantling: As 1.   Motto: Resurgam
Frame covered in black cloth
For Theophilus Richard Salwey, who d. 1837. (B.L.G. 1937 ed.)
(This hatchment is now missing, 01/90)

4. Dexter background black
Qly of sixteen, 1st, Salwey, 2nd, Washbourne, 3rd, Gules a lion rampant argent crowned or (Musard), 4th, Or on a saltire engrailed sable a bezant (Trumyn), 5th, Argent a fess sable fretty or in chief three church bells sable (Porter), 6th, Gules on a chevron between three trefoils slipped argent three roundels sable (Searle), 7th, Sable three fleurs-de-lis argent (   ), 8th, Sable a lion rampant argent a bordure engrailed or (   ), 9th, Argent three roses gules on a chief gules three quatrefoils argent (Caesar), 10th, Argent two bars sable on a chief sable three swans argent (Cesaryno), 11th, Gules three crescents argent (Perient), 12th, Azure a molet argent between three crescents or (Ryther), 13th, Vert an eagle displayed and a canton argent (Biddulph), 14th, Argent a chevron rompu between three trefoils slipped sable (   ), 15th, Argent on a chief or a fleur-de-lis gules (Rogers), 16th, Argent fretty sable a chief gules (Talmach), impaling, Gules a fess vair between three molets argent (Baugh)
Crest: A Saracen's head affronté couped at the shoulders proper the shoulders vested vert, wreathed at the temples argent and sable
Mantling: Gules and ermine   Motto: Fiat voluntas Dei   Frame covered in black cloth
For Richard Salwey, of the Moor Park, who m. Isabella, 3rd dau. of Job Walker Baugh, of Stonehouse, Salop, and d. 4 Feb. 1825.
(B.L.G. 1937 ed.)

5. All black background
On a lozenge   Salwey, impaling, Gules a fess vairy azure and sable between three molets sable pierced argent (Baugh)
Motto: In coelo quies   Frame covered in black cloth
For Isabella, widow of Richard Salwey. She d. 28 Aug. 1857.
(B.L.G. 1937 ed.; M.I. in church)

6. Dexter background black
Qly, 1st and 4th, Salwey, 2nd and 3rd, Ermine on a fess sable a castle triple-towered argent a canton gules (Hill), impaling, Qly, 1st and 4th, Argent a dexter hand within a bordure engrailed sable (Manley), 2nd and 3rd, Argent a chevron between three crescents gules (Pole)
Crest: As 1.　　Mantling: Gules and ermine　　Motto: Resurgam
Frame covered in black cloth
For Arthur Salwey, who m. 1824, Anne Frances Pole, only dau. of Vice-Admiral Manley, of Braziers, Oxon, and d. 1834.　　(B.L.G. 1937 ed.)

7. Dexter background black
Salwey, impaling, Or ermined sable on a chevron between three roses gules barbed and seeded sable two swords sable hilted or (Ricketts)
Crest: As 1., but wreathed or and sable　　Mantling: Gules and argent
Motto: Resurgam　　Frame covered in black cloth
Either for Edward Salwey, of the Lodge, Ludlow, son of Theophilus Richard Salwey, who m. 1838, Harriet Anne, eldest dau. of Thomas Bourke Ricketts, of Coombe, co. Hereford, and d. May 1840, or for John Salwey, who m. 1843, his cousin Edward's widow, and d. 21 Mar. 1871. (B.L.G. 1937 ed.)

8. All black background
Or on a pile engrailed sable three cross crosslets or in base two fountains (Hallifax), impaling, Or ermined sable on a chevron between three roses gules two swords argent hilted or (Ricketts)　　Motto: Resurgam
Shield flanked by two cherubs' heads　　Frame covered in black cloth
For the Rev. Robert Fitzwilliam Hallifax, Rector, who m. 1803, Eliza Bourke, dau. of George Crawford Ricketts, of Ashford Hall, and d. 16 July 1837. She d. 18 Apr. 1814.　　(M.I. by hatchment)

ROSS-ON-WYE (Harewood House Chapel)

1. All black background
Per pale azure and gules a chevron between three lions rampant or, in honour point the Badge of Ulster (Hoskyns), impaling, Qly ermine and gules (Stanhope)
Crest: A lion couped at the shoulders proper ducally crowned or
Mantling: Gules and argent　　Motto: Resurgam
For Sir Hungerford Hoskyns, 6th Bt., who m. 1774, Catherine, dau. of Edwyn Francis Stanhope, of Stanwell House, Middlesex, and d. 10 July 1802.　　(B.P. 1949 ed.)

2. All black background
Hoskyns, with Badge of Ulster, impaling, Qly, 1st, Per pale azure and sable a lion rampant within an orle of fleurs-de-lis or a canton ermine (Philips), 2nd and 3rd, Gules on a bend argent cotised engrailed ermine

three stags' heads cabossed gules, all between two pheons argent (Stubbs),
4th, Or a lion rampant holding a mascle gules (   )
Crest: A lion's head couped proper ducally crowned or
For Sir Hungerford Hoskyns, 7th Bt., who m. 1803, Sarah (d. 12 Mar.
1860), youngest dau. of John Philips, of Bank Hall, Lancaster, and d. 27
Feb. 1862.   (B.P. 1949 ed.)
(These two hatchments, recorded in 1952, are now missing)

SALTMARSHE Castle

1. Dexter background black

Qly, 1st and 4th, qly i. & iv. Sable a lion passant guardant between three
escallops argent (Barneby), ii. & iii. Qly or and azure four lions rampant
counterchanged (Lutley), 2nd and 3rd, Sable a chevron between three
bulls' heads cabossed argent (Bulkeley), impaling, Qly of eight, 1st and
8th, Barneby quartering Lutley, 2nd, Per pale argent and or a fess nebuly
between three lions' heads erased gules langued azure (Dance), 3rd,
Ermine a chief dancetty gules (   ), 4th, Gules a chevron between ten
crosses formy argent (Berkeley), 5th, Gules a lion rampant argent
(Mowbray), 6th, Sable a lion rampant argent crowned or (Segrave), 7th,
Gules three lions passant guardant in pale or a label of three points argent
(Brotherton)
Crest: A lion couchant guardant sable, armed and langued gules
Mantling: Gules and or   Motto: Resurgam
For William Barneby, J.P., High Sheriff 1849, who m. his cousin, Mary,
2nd dau. of Richard Barneby, of Worcester, and d. Jan. 1857.   (B.L.G.
1937 ed.)
(The whereabouts of this hatchment is unknown)

ST WEONARDS

1. Dexter background black

Per pale argent and sable a chevron between three talbots passant
counterchanged, on a chief gules three leopards' faces or (Gouge)
In pretence: Argent a fess between three lozenges azure (Parry)
Crest: A cubit arm in armour the hand grasping a dragon's head erased
breathing fire all proper   Mantling: Gules and argent   Motto:
Virtus dura vincit
For Robert Minors Gouge, of Triago, who m. Mary, dau. and heiress of
Thomas Parry, of Arkston, and d. 7 Feb. 1765, aged 43.   (Burke's
Commoners, I, 87; M.I. in church)

2. All black background

Qly of nine, 1st and 9th, Or a griffin segreant sable (Morgan), 2nd, Gules
a lion rampant or (Meredith), 3rd, Argent three bulls' heads cabossed
sable (Morgan), 4th, Sable on a mount vert a boar argent head gules
before a tree proper (Lhwarch Lhwen Vaur), 5th, Azure a chevron

Herefordshire

between three lions' heads erased or (Wyndham), 6th, Sable a fess between three boys' heads couped at the shoulders proper around each neck a snake argent (Vaughan), 7th, Or a chevron between three estoiles of six points gules (Colchester), 8th, Argent on a bend engrailed azure a cross crosslet fitchy in dexter chief argent (Clarke)   In pretence: Argent a chevron between three lozenges azure (Parry)
Crest: A stag's head couped or   Mantle: Gules and argent   Motto: In coelo quies   Winged skull in base
For Charles Morgan, of Ruperra, who m. Mary, widow of Thomas Minors Gouge, and dau. of Thomas Parry, of Arkston, and d. 24 May 1787. (B.P. 1875 ed., sub Tredegar)
(There is another hatchment for Charles Morgan at Lower Machen, Monmouth)

3. Sinister background black

Qly of twenty-four, 1st, Argent a chevron gules between three roundels azure (Baskerville), 2nd, Sable an eagle displayed or armed gules, on a chief azure within a bordure a chevron between in chief two crescents and in base a rose argent (Mynors), 3rd, Baskerville, 4th, Gules a fess chequy argent and sable between six crosses flory or (Boteler), 5th, Qly per fess indented gules and ermine a label of three points per pale or and sable (Rees), 6th, Gules a fess ermine a label of six points or (Rees ap Griffith), 7th, Qly argent and azure on a bend sable three martlets or (Le Gros), 8th, Argent two lions passant azure (Paveley), 9th, Or a chevron azure between three lions' heads erased gules (Sollers), 10th, Argent a pale sable (Erskine), 11th, Gules a fess or between three escallops argent (Pychard), 12th, Argent on a bend gules three oval buckles or (Sapie), 13th, Argent a chevron between three martlets sable (Brenton), 14th, Gules a chevron between three escallops argent (Milborne), 15th, Gules fretty ermine (Eynsford), 16th, Argent a bend between six martlets gules (Furnival), 17th, Or a fret gules (Verdon), 18th, Argent a lion rampant sable ducally crowned gules (Loveton), 19th, Baskerville, with crescent or for difference, 20th, Azure a bend cotised or between six cross crosslets fitchy argent (Blakett), 21st, Argent a griffin segreant regardant sable (Griffin ?), 22nd, Azure a fess between three chessrooks or (Bodenham), 23rd, Sable a horse's head erased between three dexter gauntlets argent (Ap Gwillim), 24th, Baskerville   In pretence: Sable a chevron between three roundels argent each charged with a cock gules (Hancock)
Motto: Resurgam   Above the shield a lover's knot and two cherubs' heads
For Anne, dau. and heiress of John Hancock of, Marlborough, who m. as his 1st wife, Thomas Baskerville Mynors-Baskerville, of Rockley House, Wilts, and Clyro Court, Radnor, and d. 13 June 1832, aged 35.   (B.L.G. 1937 ed.; M.I. in church)
(There is an identical hatchment in the parish church at Winterbourne Bassett, Wilts; her husband's hatchment is at Clyro, Radnorshire)

SARNESFIELD

1. All black background
On a lozenge suspended from a bow of white ribbon, and surrounded by sprays of white flowers   Argent a chevron between three unicorns rampant sable (Monington)
Motto: In caelo quies
For Bridget Monington, youngest dau. and co-heiress of Edward Monington, d. 1775, aged 33.   (M.I. in church)

STOKE EDITH House

1. Dexter background black (should be all black)
Argent a fess engrailed between three cinquefoils sable a bordure sable (Foley)   In pretence: Qly, 1st and 4th, Azure on a chevron between in chief three doves and in base a fleur-de-lis or three crescents vert (Hodgetts), 2nd and 3rd, Foley
Crest: A lion sejant argent holding between the forepaws an escutcheon with the arms of Foley   Mantling: Gules and argent   Motto: Resurgam
For the Hon. Edward Foley, 2nd son of Thomas, 1st Lord Foley, who m. 2nd, 1790, Eliza Maria, dau. and heir of John Hodgetts, of Prestwood, by his wife, Eliza Maria, only child of William Foley, and d. 22 June, 1808. She d. 9 July 1805.   (B.L.G. 1937 ed.)

2. Sinister background black
Qly, 1st and 4th, Foley, with a crescent for difference, 2nd and 3rd, Hodgetts, impaling, Qly, 1st, Per saltire argent and azure a saltire gules (Gage), 2nd, Argent a chevron between three talbots' heads erased sable (Hall), 3rd, Azure a sun in splendour or (St Clere), 4th, Gules a bend ermine, on a canton or a lion's head erased gules (Milbanke)
Crests: Dexter, A lion sejant argent holding between the forepaws an escutcheon with the arms of Foley   Sinister, A horse's head ermine pierced through the neck with a spear the staff broken proper   Motto: Ut prosim
For Charlotte Margaret, dau. of John Gage, of Rogate Lodge, by Mary, his wife, dau. of John Milbanke, who m. 1825, John Hodgetts Hodgetts-Foley, and d. 9 Sept. 1855.   (B.L.G. 1937 ed.)

3. All black background
Arms: as 2.
For John Hodgetts-Foley, who d. 13 Nov. 1861.   (B.L.G. 1937 ed.)
(The current whereabouts of these hatchments are unknown)

TYBERTON

1. Sinister background black
Argent on a cross sable a leopard's face or (Brydges), impaling, Argent a chevron sable between three ravens proper (Rice)   Motto: Memoria pii aeterna

Herefordshire

For Catherine, dau. of Griffith Rice, of Newton, Carmarthen, who m., as his 2nd wife, William Brydges, of Tyberton, and d.   (B.L.G. 1937 ed., sub Lee-Warner)

2. All black background
Brydges, impaling, to the dexter, Ermine a demi-lion rampant erased azure collared or the collar charged with three roundels gules (Card of Gray's Inn), and to the sinister, Argent a chevron sable between three ravens proper (Rice of Newtown)
Crest: A Saracen's head in profile couped at the shoulders, vested paly or and gules and semé of roundels counterchanged, collared ermine, wreathed at the temples argent and azure   Motto: Memoria pii aeterna   No frame
For William Brydges, of Tyberton, who m. 1st, Jane, only dau. and heir of Andrew Card, of Gray's Inn. She d. 1718. He m. 2nd, Catherine, dau. of Griffith Rice, of Newtown, Carmarthen, and d. 1764.   (B.L.G. 1937 ed.)

3. Dexter background black
Qly of six, 1st and 6th, Brydges, 2nd, Or four bars sable in chief a chessrook between two molets sable (Marshall of Blewbury), 3rd, Gules a fess between three molets or (Oswald of Strangford), 4th, Sable a fess wavy between three lions rampant or a crescent sable for difference (Kemp?), 5th, Card, impaling, Qly, 1st and 4th, Or a lion rampant sable collared and chained or (Phillipps of Eaton Bishop), 2nd and 3rd, Argent three ravens proper each standing on a mount vert (Ravenhill of Hereford)
Crest: As 2.   Motto: Resurgam
For Francis William Thomas Brydges, who m. 1785, Anne, 5th dau. of Thomas Phillipps, of Eaton Bishop, and d. 30 Nov. 1793.   (B.L.G. 1937 ed.)

4. All black background
Brydges arms only
Crest: As 2.   Motto: As 2.
Unframed
Unidentified

5. All black background
Brydges arms only
Crest: As 2., but wreathed argent and gules   Motto: In memoria pii eterna
Unidentified

6. Dexter background black
Qly of six, 1st, Gules a fess counter-compony or and azure between eight billets or (Lee), 2nd, qly i. & iv. Per pale indented argent and sable, ii. &

iii. Azure a fleur-de-lis or (Warner), 3rd, Vert a cross engrailed argent (Whetenhall), 4th, Or a fess between three wolves' heads erased sable langued gules (Howe), 5th, Vert three mulberry leaves or (Woodward), 6th, Or ermined sable three scimitars erect argent hilted gules (Howarth)
In pretence: Brydges
Crest: A squirrel sejant between two oak branches fructed proper the dexter paw grasping the dexter sprig   No mantling, but sprays of leaves to dexter and sinister of shield   Motto: Resurgam   Frame covered in velvet
For the Rev. Daniel Henry Lee-Warner, of Walsingham Abbey, who m. 1808, Ann, dau. and co-heir of Francis William Thomas Brydges, of Tyberton, and d. 1858.   (B.L.G. 1937 ed.)
(There was, until recently, when destroyed by fire, an almost identical hatchment at Little Walsingham, Norfolk)

WALFORD

1. All black background
On a lozenge   Or a fess sable ermined argent between three trefoils slipped vert (Clarke)
Motto: Mors janua vitæ   Bow of ribbon above lozenge which is flanked by palm branches
Unidentified

2. All black background
On a lozenge surmounted by a skull
Clarke arms only
No motto   Cherub's head below
Probably for Jane Clarke, the last of the family, d. 26 Apr. 1806.
(M.I. in church)

3. Dexter background black
Qly, 1st and 4th, Per pale azure and gules three lions rampant or, a crescent or for difference (Evans), 2nd, Or a fess sable ermined argent between three trefoils slipped vert (Clarke), 3rd, Vert a chevron between three fleurs-de-lis (Kyrle), impaling, Argent a fess between three buglehorns sable (Thoroton)
Crest: From an earl's coronet or a dexter arm embowed the hand proper holding a dagger argent hilted or embrued gules
For Kingsmill Evans, the Hill Court, who m. 1810, Anne Roosilia, eldest dau. of Col. Thoroton, M.P. of Flintham Hall, Notts, and d. 16 July 1851. She d. 12 Nov. 1860, aged 76.   (B.L.G. 2nd ed.; M.I. in church)

WIGMORE

1. Dexter background black
Qly, 1st and 4th, Or a chevron between three molets pierced sable (Davies), 2nd and 3rd, Qly argent and sable on a bend gules three

Herefordshire 19

martlets or (Lacy)   In pretence: Per pale or and azure three demi-lions passant counterchanged (Hamond)
Crest: On a chapeau gules turned up ermine a demi-lion or   Mantling: Gules and argent   Motto: Resurgam
For the Rt. Hon. Somerset Davies, P.C., of Croft Castle and Wigmore Hall, who m. Anne, dau. and heiress of Peter Hamond, and d.
(B.L.G. 1937 ed.)

2. Dexter background black
Argent on a fess between three crescents gules three fleurs-de-lis or (Oakeley), impaling, Per pale ermine and or a fleur-de-lis per pale or and argent on a canton azure lion passant guardant argent (Banner)
Crest: A lion rampant gules   Mantling: Gules and argent   Motto: Resurgam
For Richard Oakeley, of Pen Park, Bristol, who m. Frances Banner and d. 16 Nov. 1832.   (M.I.; Church guide)

WORMBRIDGE

1. All black background
On a lozenge   Argent on a fess sable three molets or (Clive)
In pretence: Argent three molets between two barrulets all between three martlets sable (Husbands)
For Mary, dau. and heir of Martin Husbands, of Wormbridge, who m. George Clive, of Styche, and d. 1724.   (B.L.G. 1937 ed.)

2. Dexter background black
Clive, impaling, Clive
Crest: A griffin statant argent ducally gorged gules   Mantling: Gules and argent   Motto: Mors janua vitæ
For Sir Edward Clive, who m. Judith, dau. of Rev. Benjamin Clive, and d. 21 Apr. 1771.   (B.P. 1949 ed.; M.I. in church; D.N.B.)

3. All black background
Qly, 1st and 4th, Clive, 2nd and 3rd, Or on a chevron gules three lions passant guardant or (Bolton)   In pretence: Azure three arrows, 2 and 1, points downwards or (Archer)
Crest and mantling: As 2.   Motto: Audacter et sincere
For Edward Bolton Clive, of Whitfield, who m. 1790, Harriet, dau. and co-heir of Andrew, last Baron Archer, and d. 22 July 1845.   (B.L.G. 1937 ed.)

4. Sinister background black
Clive   In pretence: Paly of eight embattled argent and gules (Wigley)
Lover's knot above and palm branches flanking shield

For Caroline, dau. and co-heir of Edmund Meysey Wigley, of Shakenhurst, Worcs, who m. 1840, the Rev. Archer Clive, of Whitfield, and d. 13 July 1873.   (B.L.G. 1937 ed.; M.I. in church)

5. All black background
Clive with crescent or for difference   In pretence: Wigley
Crest and motto: As 3.   Mantling: Sable and argent
For the Rev. Archer Clive, who d. 17 Sept. 1878.   (B.L.G. 1937 ed.)

SHROPSHIRE

Great Ness 1: For John Edwards, 1850
(*Photograph by Mr. J. E. Titterton*)

INTRODUCTION

With just on 200 hatchments Shropshire has one of the highest concentrations in the survey. One quarter of these are (or were) to be found in the County Town of Shrewsbury. Shrewsbury New St Chads had 21 hatchments and the Old St Chads building had 20 recorded. One wonders if all 41 would have survived if the Old Church had not collapsed and was still the parish church. The hatchment which has been used for the front cover illustration of this volume and all of the series is to be found in New St Chads (No. 3).

There are a number of 17th-century hatchments. Only one, (No. 1 at St Julian, Shrewsbury) is identified. Those at Chirbury, Loppington, Shifnal and Water Upton, from their size, are almost certainly similarly dated. The arms at Shifnal are quarterly of six but with only two coats of Moreton and Hamer repeated! The three early Corbet hatchments in Old St Chads display the quarterly coat of 22 as given in the published *County Visitation* of 1623. One has an additional 23rd quartering of Humfreston and the initials S.V.C.K. The initials suggest it is for Sir Vincent Corbet, Knight but his wife was the Humfreston heiress. Their descendants christened Vincent were all Baronets not knights and if it is for Sir Vincent Kt. then this hatchment is earlier than the 'earliest' identified at Eye, Herefordshire. In contrast two new hatchments have been erected at Pitchford since the others in that church were first recorded.

Prominent Shropshire County families are represented several times. The best family collection is the seven hatchments for the Mytton family at Halston Hall (not accessible to the public). The Barons Forester are at Willey, Bicton and Barrow. Three other families are so well represented that their hatchments illustrate several means of differencing arms to distinguish junior branches.

The Leighton hatchments at New St Chads have a crescent to difference their arms from the family of Leighton Baronets whose hatchments are at Alderbury. The main family of Hill of Court Hill died out in 1776. There were four hatchments to this family at Nash. These have been recently restored at Attingham Park by the National

Trust. Attingham Park was the home of the Barons Berwick who were descended in the female line (but not through an heiress) from the Hill of Court Hill and assumed the surname Hill. The hatchments of three Barons Berwick at Atcham show the Hill arms differenced by a canton gules charged with a martlet or. Finally at Berwick church the hatchment of Sir Francis Brian Hill has the main Hill arms differenced by a martlet. Sir Francis was the fifth son of Sir John Hill, 3rd Bt., but as an elder brother predeceased him without issue (aged 47) he must have changed his difference mark to that of a fourth son.

Both the Leighton and Hill differencings related to descendants of a common ancestor living in the 17th century. The different branches of the Corbet family go back earlier. The hatchments at Old St Chads bear 'or a corbie sable'. At Battlefield the arms are 'or two corbies sable' which is further differenced at Longnor by a bordure engrailed gules bezanty.

Thanks are due to many people who have been involved in the Shropshire survey. Most of the hatchments were recorded in the 1950s by Mr. A. L. Le Quesne, Mr. A. J. Langdon and Mr. G. A. Harrison (who also produced the front cover illustration referred to above). The majority were checked by the late Mr. W. A. Peplow. Mr. Michael Holmes of Shrewsbury also rendered valuable assistance.

JOHN E. TITTERTON
7 Cecil Aldin Drive, Tilehurst, Reading

ACTON SCOTT
1. Dexter background black
Qly, 1st, Argent three saltires raguly gules in chief a stackhouse sable and in base a garb azure, in dexter chief a crescent for difference (Stackhouse), 2nd, Argent a greyhound courant gules between three roundels gules (Courtenay), 4th, Sable a falcon between three molets or (Pendarves)   In pretence: Qly, 1st and 4th, Gules two lions passant argent between nine cross crosslets or (Acton), 2nd and 3rd, Or two bars and in chief a lion passant azure (Gregory)
Crest: A saltire reguly or   Motto: Resurgam
For John Stackhouse, who m. 1773, Susanna, only dau. and heiress of Edward Acton, and d. 22 Nov. 1819.   (B.L.G. 5th ed.)

2. All black background
On a lozenge surmounted by a cherub's head
Arms: As 1.
For Susanna, widow of John Stackhouse, d. 1834.   (B.L.G. 5th ed.)

3. Dexter background black
Qly, 1st and 4th, Acton, as 1., 2nd, Qly per fess indented argent and gules in the first quarter a raven proper (Acton), 3rd, Stackhouse, impaling, Argent three pallets gules within a bordure engrailed azure, on a canton gules a spur or (Knight)
Crest: A human leg in armour couped at the thigh and flexed at the knee argent, spurred and garnished or   Mantling: Gules and argent
Motto: Mors janua vitæ
For Thomas Pendarves Stackhouse-Acton, who m. 1812, Frances, dau. of Thomas Andrew Knight, of Downton Castle, and d.   (B.L.G. 5th ed.)

ALBERBURY
1. All black background
Ermine on a fess sable three molets argent (Lyster)   To dexter of main shield: Lyster, impaling, Azure two bars wavy argent, on a chief or a demi-lion rampant sable (Smyth) A.B1.   To sinister of main shield: Lyster, impaling, Sable a lion rampant argent (   ) D.B1.
Crest: A stag's head proper   Mantling: Gules and argent   Motto: Resurgemus
Probably for Richard Lyster, who m. Mary, dau. of Moses Smith, and d. 14 Apr. 1794.   (B.L.G. 2nd ed.)

2. All black background

Qly of six, 1st, Lyster, 2nd, Argent a chevron between three dolphins sable ( ), 3rd, Argent on a bend gules three molets argent a bordure gules ( ), 4th, Gules three lions rampant or ( ), 5th, Argent a bend sable a chief chequy gules and or (for Fitz-Herbert), 6th, Argent on a bend sable three dragon flies argent ( ), impaling, Argent two trefoils slipped sable a chief gules (Rodd)
Crest and mantling: As 1.   Motto: Loyal au mort
For Richard Lyster, who m. Mary, dau. of the Rev. John Rodd, and d. 23 May 1807.   (B.L.G. 2nd ed.)

3. Dexter background black

Qly of six, as 2., impaling, Gules a chevron between three spearheads argent (Price)
Crest, mantling and motto: As 2.
For Richard Lyster, who m. 1794, Penelope Anne, dau. of Henry Price, of Knighton, and d. 3 May 1819.   (B.L.G. 2nd ed.)

4. All black background

Qly per fess indented or and gules, in chief the Badge of Ulster (Leighton)
Crest: A wyvern wings expanded sable   Mantling: Gules and argent
Motto: Dread shame
For Sir Charlton Leighton, 4th Bt., d. 9 Sept. 1784, or Sir Robert Leighton, 5th Bt., d. Feb. 1819.   (B.P. 1965 ed.)

5. Exactly as last, but larger

For Sir Charlton Leighton, 4th Bt., d. 9 Sept. 1784, or Sir Robert Leighton, 5th Bt., d. Feb. 1819.   (B.P. 1965 ed.)

6. Dexter 2/3 background black

Leighton, as 4., impaling, to the dexter, Ermine three lozenges conjoined in fess sable (Pigott), and to the sinister, Argent on a bend azure three stags' heads cabossed or (Stanley)
Crest, mantling and motto: As 4.
For Sir Baldwin Leighton, 6th Bt., who m. 1st, 1780, Anna, dau. of the Rev. William Pigott, Rector of Edmond, and 2nd, 1802, Margaretta Louisa Anne (d. 8 Jan. 1842), dau. of Sir John Thomas Stanley, Bt., of Adderley Park, co. Chester, and d. 13 Nov. 1828.   (B.P. 1965 ed.)

7. Dexter background black

Leighton, as 4., impaling, Sable a cross floretty between four escallops argent (Fletcher)
Crest: A wyvern proper wings gules   Mantling and motto: As 4.
For Sir Bryan Baldwin Mawddwy Leighton, 9th Bt., who m. 1890, Margaret Frances, dau. of Major John Fletcher, of Saltoun Hall, co. Haddington, and d. 19 Jan. 1919.   (B.P. 1965 ed.)

ASTON HALL

1. All black background
Qly, 1st and 4th, Per fess sable and argent a lion rampant counterchanged (Lloyd), 2nd and 3rd, Qly or and sable in each quarter a stag trippant counterchanged (Lloyd), impaling, Argent a scythe and at fess point a fleur-de-lis sable (Sneyd)
Crest: From a ducal coronet a demi-lion rampant argent   Mantling: Gules and argent   Motto: In coelo quies
In poor condition, torn and patched
For the Rev. William Lloyd, of Aston, who m. 1757, Elizabeth, elder dau. of William Sneyd, of Biston, Staffs, and d. 11 June 1774.   (B.L.G. 1937 ed.)

2. Dexter background black
Qly, 1st and 4th, Per fess sable and argent a lion rampant counterchanged (Lloyd), 2nd, Qly or and sable in each quarter a stag trippant counterchanged (Lloyd), 3rd, Argent on a fess gules between three cinquefoils sable a greyhound courant or (Albany)   In pretence: Or on a chief indented sable three crescents argent (Harvey)
Crest, mantling and motto: As 1.
For William Lloyd, J.P., D.L., of Aston Hall, who m. Louisa, dau. and coheir of Admiral Sir E. Harvey, and d. 20 Apr. 1843.   (B.L.G. 5th ed.)

ATCHAM

1. Sinister background black
Or three bars azure, on a bend gules three roses argent (Lingen), impaling, Ermine on a fess azure a castle argent (Hill)
Crest: Five leeks proper encircled with a ducal coronet or
For Anne, dau. of Thomas Hill, of Tern Hall, who m. 1748, Robert Burton (formerly Lingen), of Longner, and d. 30 Apr. 1771, aged 40. (B.L.G. 1937 ed.; inscr. on hatchment frame)

2. All black background
Qly, 1st and 4th, Per pale azure and purpure a cross engrailed or between four roses argent (Burton), 2nd and 3rd, Barry of six or and azure on a bend gules three roses argent (Lingen), impaling, Ermine on a fess sable a castle with two towers argent (Hill)
Crest: A dexter gauntlet couped at the wrist proper   Mantling: Gules and argent   Motto: Dominus providebit   Skull in base
For Robert Burton (formerly Lingen), of Longner, who d. 21 June 1803, aged 75.   (Sources, as 1.)

3. All black background
Qly, as 2., impaling, Gules on a fess between three goats' heads erased argent three roundels sable (Gittins)

Crests: Dexter, as 2.   Sinister, as 1.   Mantling and motto: As 2.
For the Rev. Henry Burton, Vicar of Atcham, who m. Mary, dau. of
William Gittins, of Chilton, and d. 16 Jan. 1831.   (B.L.G. 1937 ed.)

4. Sinister background black
Qly of twelve, 1st, qly i. & iv. Azure a cross engrailed or between four
roses argent (Burton), ii. & iii. Or three bars azure on a bend gules three
roses argent (Lingen), 2nd, Azure a chevron ermine between three fleurs-
de-lis argent (Burgh), 3rd, Or a lion rampant gules a bordure wavy sable
(Mouthe), 4th, qly i. & iv. Argent two bars gules fretty argent (Clopton),
ii. & iii. Gules a fess between six pears or (Clopton), 5th, Or a raven
sable (Corbet), 6th, Or an escarbuncle sable (Turet), 7th, Sable a double-
headed eagle displayed within a bordure wavy argent (Milewater), 8th,
Burton, 9th, Gules on a bend argent a lion passant sable (Madocks), 10th,
Gules three sheaves of arrows or (Biest), 11th, Per pale gules and sable a
lion rampant argent (Ballard), 12th, Sable a lion rampant argent
(Matthews)   In pretence: Qly, 1st, Vert three eagles wings displayed
argent (Smitheman), 2nd, Chequy argent and sable (Brooke), 3rd, Gules a
talbot passant or (   ), 4th, Azure semy-de-lis a lion rampant or
(Dalton)
For Rose, 2nd dau. and co-heir of John Smitheman, of Little Wenlock,
who m. 1798, Robert Burton, of Longner, and d.   (B.L.G. 1937 ed.)

5. All black background
Arms: As 4.
Crests, mantling and motto: As 3.
For Robert Burton, of Longner, who d.   1841.   (B.L.G. 1937 ed.)
(There is also a rectangular panel with the same arms, but with the
Smitheman eagles collared or; this panel gives identifications of the
quarterings)

6. All black background
Arms: Qly of twelve, as 4.   To dexter of main shield, Burton,
impaling, Azure a chevron ermine between three chessrooks argent
(Walcot) S.B1.   To sinister of main shield, Burton, impaling Argent on
a fess between three crescents gules three fleurs-de-lis or (Oakeley)
Crest, mantling and motto: As 3.
For Robert Burton, of Longner, who m. 1st, 1825, Catherine (d. 1830),
dau. of William Walcot, of Moor Hall, and 2nd, 1835, Catherine, dau. of
the Rev. Herbert Oakeley, of Oakeley, and d. 14 Sept. 1860.   (B.L.G.
1937 ed.)

7. All black background
Ermine on a fess azure a castle argent, on a canton gules a martlet or
(Hill), impaling to the dexter, Or a lion's gamb erased between two cross

crosslets fitchy gules (Powys), and to the sinister, Or fretty gules a canton ermine (Noel)
Crest: A tower argent   Mantling: Gules and argent   Motto: Memento mori   Two cherubs' heads above
For Thomas Hill, son of Thomas Harwood, who m. 1st, Anne, only dau. of Richard Powys, and 2nd, Mary, dau. and co-heir of William Noel, and d. June 1782. She d. 14 Feb. 1760.   (G.E.C.)

8. All black background
Qly, 1st, qly i. & iv. Hill, ii. & iii. Argent a chevron between three stags' heads cabossed gules (Harwood), 2nd, Noel, 3rd, Gules on a chief indented sable three martlets or (Lovelace), 4th, Sable a chevron between three leopards' faces or (Wentworth), impaling, Argent a lion rampant and a canton sable (Owen)
Baron's coronet   Crest: On the battlements of a tower argent a hind proper collared and chained or   Mantling: Gules and argent   Motto: Qui uti scit ei bona   Supporters: Dexter, A pegasus argent gorged with a collar gules charged with three martlets or   Sinister, A stag proper gorged with a collar sable charged with three leopards' faces or, and chained or
For Richard, 4th Baron Berwick, who m. 1800, Frances Maria, dau. of William Mostyn Owen, M.P., for Montgomery, and d. 28 Sept. 1848. (B.P. 1939 ed.)

9. Identical to 8., but no impalement
Probably for Richard, 5th Baron Berwick, who d. unm. 12 Apr. 1861. (B.P. 1939 ed.)

10. Identical to 9.
Probably for William, 6th Baron Berwick, who d. unm. 24 Nov. 1882. (B.P. 1939 ed.)

BARROW

1. All black background
Qly, 1st and 4th, Qly per fess indented argent and sable in the first and fourth quarters a hunting horn sable (Forester), 2nd and 3rd, Azure a fess embattled counter-embattled between three crescents argent (Weld)
Baron's coronet   Crests: Dexter, A talbot statant argent collared and pendent therefrom a hunting horn sable   Sinister, A wyvern sable winged or   Motto: Semper eadem   Supporters: Two talbots argent langued gules collared sable pendent therefrom a hunting horn chained or
All on a mantle gules and ermine
Unidentified

BASCHURCH

1. All black background
Sable a lion rampant argent debruised by a bend chequy or and gules (Presland)
No crest, mantling or motto   Cherub's head in top angle
Probably for the Rev. Thomas Presland, of Walford, who d. 17 Sept. 1803, aged 35.   (M.I.)

2. All black background
Per pale argent and sable a saltire counterchanged (Hunt), impaling, Sable a chevron embattled or between three roses argent barbed and seeded proper, a crescent for difference (Cornish)
Crest: A talbot sejant sable collared or, in the dexter paw a battleaxe erect or   Mantling: Gules and argent   Motto: In coelo quies
For Rowland Hunt, who m. 1781, Susannah Ann, dau. of Mark Cornish, and d. 6 July 1811.   (B.L.G. 1937 ed.)

3. Dexter background black
Hunt, impaling, Or a lion rampant reguardant sable (Lloyd)
Crest: A talbot sejant sable collared and chained or, the chain tied to a halbert in pale or headed azure with a bow azure   Mantling: Gules and argent   Motto: In coelo quies
For Rowland Hunt, of Boreatton, who m. 1823, Mary, dau. of Thomas Lloyd, of Shrewsbury, and d. Feb. 1835.   (B.L.G. 1937 ed.)

4. All black background
Vert on a fess between three greyhounds' heads erased argent three crosses formy gules (Muckleston)
Crest: A greyhound's head erased argent   Mantling: Gules and argent   Motto: In coelo quies
Probably for Joseph Muckleston, of Prescott, who d. 11 Nov. 1831, aged 76. (M.I.)

5. All black background
On a lozenge   Muckleston, impaling, Presland
For Frances, dau. of Thomas Presland, who m. William Hawkins Muckleston, M.D., of London, and d. 31 July 1837, aged 75.   (M.I.)

6. Sinister background black
Gules a bend between three martlets or (Slaney)   In pretence: Muckleston
Crest: A demi-griffin gules beaked and winged or   Mantling and motto: As 4.

For Elizabeth, only child of William Hawkins Muckleston, who m. as his 1st wife, Robert Aglionby Slaney, of Hatton Grange and Walford Manor, and d. 20 July 1847.   (B.L.G. 1937 ed.; M.I.)

7. All black background
Argent a chevron gules between three closed helmets proper (Basnett)
Crest: An arm in armour embowed holding a cutlass proper   Mantling: Gules and argent   Motto: In coelo quies   Skull in base
For the Rev. John Basnett, of Cloughs, who d. 27 Mar. 1844, aged 81. (M.I.)

BATTLEFIELD

1. Sinister background black
Or two ravens in pale proper (Corbet), impaling, Qly per fess indented or and gules (Leighton)
Cherub's head above and skull below   Motto: In coelo quies
For Emma Elizabeth, dau. of Sir Charlton Leighton, 3rd Bt., who m. as his 1st wife, John Corbet, of Sundorne, and d. 19 Sept. 1797.
(B.L.G. 1937 ed.)

2. All black background
On a lozenge   Corbet, impaling, Ermine three fusils conjoined in fess sable (Pigott)
Cherub's head in each side angle and in base
For Anne, dau. of the Rev. William Pigott, of Edgmond, who m. as his 2nd wife, John Corbet, of Sundorne, and d. 12 Dec. 1848.   (B.L.G. 1937 ed.; M.I.)

BENTHALL

1. All black background
Sable three lions passant in bend between four bendlets argent in sinister chief a trefoil slipped argent (Browne)
Crest: A griffin's head sable charged with a bar gemel and a trefoil argent
Mantling: Gules and argent   Motto: Virtus pro pyramide
Unidentified

2. All black background
Or a lion rampant double-queued azure crowned and langued gules (Benthall)
Crest: From a ducal coronet or a leopard argent spotted sable
Mantling: Gules and argent
Possibly for Richard Benthall who d. 1720.   (family)

BERRINGTON

1. All black background
Azure a fess dancetty ermine between three moors' heads proper, wreathed at the temples argent and azure (Williams ?), impaling, Argent a cinquefoil azure (Mytton)
Crest: A moor's head proper wreathed argent and azure   Mantling: Gules and argent   Motto: Mors Janua vitæ
Probably for Edward Williams, of Eaton Mascott, who m. Barbara Letitia, dau. of John Mytton of Halston, and d.   (B.L.G. 2nd ed.)

2. Sinister background black
Williams, as 1.   In pretence: Per bend sinister ermine and sable ermined argent a lion rampant or (Hosier)   Lover's knot above
For Rebekah Gillam, dau. and heiress of John Hosier, who m. Richard Williams, and d. 17 Oct. 1827, aged 50.   (M.I.)

3. All black background
Gules a chevron ermine between three men's heads affronté couped at the shoulders proper (Williams)   In pretence: Qly, 1st and 4th, Hosier, 2nd and 3rd, Azure a chevron or between three lions passant guardant argent (   )
Crest: A man's head affronté couped at the shoulders proper
Mantling: Gules and argent
For Richard Williams, who d. 22 Sept. 1831.   (M.I.)

4. Dexter background black
Qly, 1st and 4th, Hosier, 2nd and 3rd, Williams, as 3., impaling, Gules a chevron between three lions rampant or (   )
Crests: Dexter, A man's head couped at the shoulders proper   Sinister, On a chapeau gules and ermine a wyvern argent   Motto: Resurgam
Unidentified

BERWICK

1. All black background
On a lozenge with a cherub's head in each corner
Or a lion's gamb erased in bend between two cross crosslets fitchy gules (Powys), impaling, Ermine on a fess azure three molets or (Lyster)
For Jane, dau. of Thomas Lyster, who m. John Powys, and d. 1753.
(B.L.G. 2nd ed.)

2. Dexter background black
Powys, impaling, Argent a chevron between three crescents gules (Pole)
Crest: A lion's gamb erect and erased gules grasping a fleur-de-lis or

Shropshire

Mantling: Gules and argent   Motto: In coelo quies
For Thomas Powys, who m. 1756, Mary, dau. of German Pole, and d. 1774.   (B.L.G. 2nd ed.)

3. All black background
Qly of six, 1st and 6th, Powys, 2nd, Argent a saltire sable (Baldwyn), 3rd, Barry of six argent and azure a chief ermine (Wigley), 4th, Gules a chevron engrailed ermine between three eagles close argent (Child), 5th, Gules a cross argent (   )
Crest and mantling: As 2.   Motto: Parta tueri
Possibly for Thomas Henry Powys, son of No 4, who pre-deceased his father, d. unm.   (B.L.G. 2nd ed.)

4. Dexter background black
Qly of six, as 3.   In pretence: Azure a bend between two doves argent (for Cooper)
Crest and mantling: As 2.   Motto: Mors janua vitæ   Skull in base
For Thomas Jelf Powys, who m. Lissey Anne, dau. and heiress of Thomas Cooper, and d. 28 Jan. 1805.   (B.L.G. 2nd ed.; M.I.)

5. All black background
On a lozenge surmounted by two cherubs' heads
Powys   In pretence: Cooper
For Lissey Anne, widow of Thomas Jelf Powys, who d. 14 July 1832. (Sources, as 4.)

6. All black background
Ermine on a fess sable a castle triple-towered argent, in chief a martlet gules for difference (Hill)   In pretence: Qly, 1st and 4th, Powys, 2nd and 3rd, Cooper
Crest: A castle triple-towered argent surmounted by two sprays of laurel slipped and leaved proper   Mantling: Gules and argent   Motto: Avancez   Below the motto an Order on a ribbon, inscribed: PORTUG. P. BRASI. JOAN. D. G. REG.
For Sir Francis Brian Hill, of Preston Montford, who m. 2nd, 1819, Emily Lissey (d. 13 Feb. 1840), dau. of Thomas Jelf Powys, and d. 4 Apr. 1842. (B.P. 1965 ed.)

BETTON STRANGE

1. Dexter background black
Argent three Catherine wheels sable a bordure engrailed gules (Scott), impaling, Qly, 1st, Ermine on a saltire gules a crescent or for difference (Wynne), 2nd, Vert three eagles displayed in fess or (Owen Gwynedd),

3rd, Argent two foxes counter-salient in saltire gules (Williams), 4th, Gules a lion rampant reguardant or (   )
Crest: A demi-griffin proper beaked and legged or   Mantling: Gules and argent   Motto: Recte faciendo neminum timent
For George Jonathan Scott, who m. 1840, Augusta Frances, dau. of William Wynne, and d. 1875. She d. 1901.   (B.L.G. 1937 ed.)

BICTON

1. Dexter background black

Qly per fess indented argent and sable four bugle-horns counterchanged, a crescent for difference (Forester), impaling, Azure a chevron ermine between three escallops argent (Townshend)
Crest: A talbot passant argent collared and chained or   Mantling: Gules and argent   Motto: In coelo quies   No frame
For Cecil Forester, 2nd son of William Forester, who m. Anne, dau. and co-heiress of Robert Townshend, and d. 22 Aug. 1774.   (B.P. 1965 ed.)
(This hatchment, recorded in poor condition in 1954, is now missing)

BOURTON

1. Dexter background black

Qly, 1st and 4th, Argent a cross formy extended to the sides of the shield chequy sable and or (Lawley), 2nd, Argent on a fess engrailed sable between three lions' heads erased gules three bezants (Ringley), 3rd, Qly ermine and gules a bordure engrailed azure (   ), over all the Badge of Ulster, impaling, Argent a bend sable between in chief a unicorn's head erased and in base a cross crosslet fitchy gules (Denison)
Baron's coronet   Crest: A wolf passant sable langued gules   Motto: Pro jure populi   Supporters: Two wolves sable langued gules collared or pendent therefrom each an escutcheon, Argent a chevron between three Moors' heads erased sable
For Robert, 1st Baron Wenlock, who m. 1793, Maria, dau. of Joseph Denison, and d.s.p. 10 Apr. 1832.   (B.P. 1875 ed.)

BURFORD

1. All black background

Qly, 1st and 4th, Per fess azure and gules three cups or in each a boar's head erect argent (Bowles), 2nd and 3rd, Sable two lions passant guardant in pale a bordure engrailed or (Rushout), impaling, Or a fess chequy argent and azure, over all a bend engrailed gules, a double tressure flory counterflory gules (Stewart)
Crests: Dexter, A demi-boar or ermined sable, crined unguled and bristled or, pierced through the chest with an arrow or headed argent   Sinister, A lion passant guardant or   Mantling: Gules and argent   Motto: Resurgam

Shropshire

For the Rev. George Rushout-Bowles, who m. 1803, Caroline, dau. of John, 7th Earl of Galloway, and d. Oct. 1842.   (B.P. 1875 ed.)

2. Dexter background black
Sable two lions passant guardant in pale a bordure engrailed or, the Badge of Ulster (Rushout), impaling, Qly, 1st and 4th, Or a bend engrailed vert cotised sable a crescent sable charged with a crescent argent for difference (Hanbury), 2nd and 3rd, Or on a fess sable between three Muscovy ducks proper a rose or (Bateman)
Baron's coronet   Crest: A lion passant guardant or   Motto: Par ternis suppar   Supporters: Two angels proper winged and crined or habited argent semy of fleurs-de-lis and molets or, sashed azure, in the exterior hand a palm branch vert
For George, 3rd Baron Northwick, who m. 1869, Elizabeth Augusta, dau. of William, 1st Lord Bateman, and d. 11 Nov. 1887.   (G.E.C.)

CHIRBURY

1. All black background
Qly per fess indented azure and gules three lions rampant or, a crescent for difference (   )
Crest: Not discernible   Mantling: Gules and argent   Motto: Virescit vulnere virtus
In very poor condition
Unidentified

2. Dexter background black
Qly, 1st and 4th, Gules on a bend argent a lion passant sable (Davies), 2nd, Argent a lion passant sable a bordure indented gules (   ), 3rd, Azure three lions rampant or on a chief argent three cross crosslets sable (Mathew), impaling, Qly, 1st and 4th, Gules a talbot passant argent a chief ermine (for Butt), 2nd and 3rd, Argent on a bend azure three martlets or (   )
Crest: A lion's head argent ducally crowned gules   Mantling: Gules and argent   Motto: In coelo quies
For John Davies, of Marrington Hall, who m. Charlotte, dau. of Peter Butt, of Deptford, and d. 1842. She d. 1872.   (M.I.)

3. Dexter background black
Qly, 1st, Argent a lion passant sable between three fleurs-de-lis gules (Pryce), 2nd, Argent on a bend sable between two crescents gules three annulets or (Evan ap Rhys), 3rd, Sable three nags' heads erased argent (Lloyd), 4th, Argent three boars' heads couped sable (Evan ap Rhys ap Hugo), impaling, Or
Crest: A demi-lion rampant sable in the paws a fleur-de-lis or

Mantling: Gules and argent   Motto: In coelo quies
For Richard Pryce of Gunley and Lincolns Inn, who d. 1706.
(Inscription under hatchment)

4. All black background
Qly, 1st and 4th, Pryce, as 3., 2nd and 3rd, Argent a chevron between three swans' necks erased sable (Bransby), impaling, Gules a falcon argent wings elevated argent in the dexter claw a martlet or, all within a bordure engrailed or (Edwards)
Crest: A demi-lion rampant sable in the paws a fleur-de-lis or   Motto: In coelo quies
For Richard Pryce, of Gunley, who m. 1795, Eliza Constantia, youngest dau. of the Rev. Samuel d'Elboeuf Edwards, of Pentre, and d. 26 Oct. 1832.   (B.L.G. 5th ed.)

5. All black background
Qly, 1st and 4th, Argent a cross flory sable the ends or (Newton), 2nd, Argent on a bend sable three martlets argent (Hinton), 3rd, Sable in chief three fleurs-de-lis argent (   ), impaling, Argent on a fess between three crescents gules three fleurs-de-lis or (Oakeley)
Crest: An eagle's leg sable entwined with a snake or   Mantling: Gules and argent
An inscription on scroll below shield, almost illegible, but date visible 16 March 1681.
Unidentified
(This hatchment was reported as missing in 1979)

CLAVERLEY

1. All black background
On a lozenge surmounted by a cherub's head
Qly, 1st and 4th, Argent a double-headed eagle displayed sable (Glynne), 2nd and 3rd, Argent three brands raguly sable inflamed proper (   ), in centre chief the Badge of Ulster   In pretence: Gules on a fess between three demi-lions rampant or three roundels azure (Bennet)
Skull in base
For Mary, only dau. and heir of Richard Bennet, of Farmcot, who m. the Rev. Sir Stephen Glynn, 7th Bt., and d.   He d. Apr. 1780.   (B.P. 1868 ed.)

2. Sinister background black
Qly gules and ermine in the second and third quarters three piles gules over all on a fess azure five bezants (Gatacre)   In pretence: Qly, 1st and 4th, Qly or and gules four lions passant counterchanged (Lloyd), 2nd and 3rd, Azure a fess ermine between three lions rampant or (   )

Shropshire

For Annabella, dau. and co-heir of Robert Lloyd, of Swanhill, who m. 1805, as his 1st wife, Edward Gatacre, and d. 17 Feb. 1817. (B.L.G. 1937 ed.; M.I.)

3. Dexter background black
Gatacre   In pretence: Lloyd   Also impaling, Or a lion rampant reguardant sable (Jenkins)
To dexter of main shield, Gatacre with Lloyd in pretence S.B1.   To sinister of main shield, Gatacre impaling Jenkins D.B1.
Crest: A raven proper   Mantling: Gules and argent   Motto: In coelo quies   Cherub's head below
For Edward Gatacre, who m. 1st, Annabella, dau. and co-heir of Robert Lloyd, and 2nd, 1826, Harriet Constantia, eldest dau. of Richard Jenkins, of Bicton, and d. 24 Nov. 1849.   (B.L.G. 1937 ed.; M.I.)

4. All black background
On a lozenge   Qly, 1st and 4th, Argent an eagle displayed gules armed or, on a chief sable three bezants each charged with a fleur-de-lis azure (Grazebrook), 2nd and 3rd, qly i. & iv. Per pale sable and or a chevron between three escallops counterchanged (Worrall), ii. Qly per fess indented sable and or (   ), iii. Gules a lion rampant argent (   )
In pretence: Qly, 1st and 4th, Paly of eight or and gules on a chief argent three lozenges gules (Wilkes), 2nd and 3rd, Azure a garb or (Grosvenor)
For Elizabeth, only dau. and heir of Robert Wilkes, of Dallicott House, who m. 1805, Thomas Worrall Grazebrook, and d. 18 June 1837. (B.L.G. 1937 ed.; M.I.)

5. All black background
Qly, 1st, Grazebrook, 2nd, Wilkes, 3rd, Grosvenor, 4th, Worrall
Crest: A bear's head erased or muzzled sable   Mantling: Gules and argent   Mottoes: (above crest) Forbear   (below shield) I know that my redeemer liveth   Cherub's head below
For Thomas Worrall Smith Grazebrook, who d. unm. 1 Aug. 1846. (B.L.G. 1937 ed.; M.I.)

CLEOBURY NORTH
1. All black background
Qly, 1st and 4th, Per pale azure and gules a double-headed eagle displayed or a bordure engrailed argent (Mytton), 2nd and 3rd, Argent a chevron between three heronshaws sable (Henshaw)
No mantling, helm or motto
Crest: A bull's head couped sable armed or charged with three annulets or   Winged cherub's head in base
Probably for Thomas Mytton, who d. unm. 1818.   (B.L.G. 5th ed.)

2. All black background
On a lozenge   Arms: As 1.
Probably for Harriett Mytton, who d. unm. 1859.   (B.L.G. 5th ed.)

CLUNGUNFORD
1. Dexter background black
Qly, 1st and 4th, two coats per pale, Gules a lion rampant reguardant argent (Lloyd), Argent three boars' heads sable (   ), 2nd, Gules a fess sable between six cross crosslets fitchy argent (   ), 3rd, Sable a double-headed eagle displayed or (   ), impaling, Or a saltire gules (Eustace) Knight's helm   Crest: From a ducal coronet or an eagle's head azure beaked or   Mantling: Gules and argent   Motto: Resurgam
For Gen. Sir Evan Lloyd, of Ferney Hall, who m. Alicia Eustace, and d. 1846.   (B.L.G. 2nd ed.)

2. Dexter background black
Or three chessrooks sable a chief embattled sable (Rocke), impaling, Sable on a chevron between three griffins' heads erased or three estoiles gules (Beale)
Crest: On a rock proper a martlet or   Mantling: Gules   Motto: Resurgam
For the Rev. John Rocke, who m. 1812, Anne, dau. of Thomas Beale, of Heath House, and d. 14 Jan. 1849.   (B.L.G. 5th ed.)

COUND
1. All black background
On a lozenge   Qly, 1st and 4th, Argent chevron between three lions rampant sable (Thursby), 2nd and 3rd, Or a chevron between three leopards' faces gules (Harvey)   In pretence: Qly, 1st and 4th, qly i. & iv. Azure three pelicans vulning themselves proper, ii. & iii. Gules two demi-belts in pale argent with buckles and studs or (Pelham), 2nd, Azure a cross within a bordure engrailed or (Cresset), 3rd, Argent on a bend cotised gules three crescents argent (Huxley)
For Frances, eldest dau. and co-heir of Henry Pelham, of Cound Hall, who m. 1800, the Rev. George August Thursby, Rector of Abington, Northants, and d. 12 Mar. 1852.   (B.L.G. 5th ed.; M.I.)

CULMINGTON
1. Dexter background black
Argent a saltire sable on a chief gules three cushions or (Johnstone), impaling, a blank (argent)
Crest: A winged spur or   Mantling: Gules and argent   Motto: Nunquam no paratus
Unidentified

Shropshire 39

DIDDLEBURY

1. Dexter background black
Qly, 1st and 4th, Ermine a lion rampant gules ducally crowned or a bordure sable bezanty (Cornewall), 2nd, Per pale azure and gules three lions rampant argent (Herbert), 3rd, Gules a cross raguly between four leopards' heads erased argent (Walker)
Crest: A chough proper   Mantling: Gules and argent   Motto: Semper pro patria
For Frederick Cornewall, M.P. for Ludlow, who d.s.p. 1783, or, more probably on stylistic grounds, for Herbert Cornewall, who m. Charlotte, dau. of Gen. Lord Charles Somerset, and d. 1863.   (B.L.G. 5th ed.)

2. Sinister background black
Argent ten roundels, four, three, two and one gules (See of Worcester), impaling, Qly, as 1.
Shield surmounted by a bishop's mitre
For the Rt. Rev. Folliot Herbert Walker Cornewall, D.D., Bishop of Worcester, who m. Anne, dau. of the Hon. George Hamilton, and d. 5 Sept. 1831, aged 77.   (B.L.G. 5th ed.)

DITTON PRIORS

1. Sinister background black
Qly, 1st and 4th, qly, i. & iv. Gules three cinquefoils argent (Hamilton), ii. & iii. Argent a lymphad sable (Arran), 2nd, qly, i. & iv. Azure three molets or between nine cross crosslets fitchy three, three and three argent (Somerville), ii. & iii. Argent a cross crosslet sable (   ), 3rd, Sable three boys' heads couped at the shoulders proper about each neck a serpent or (Vaughan)   In pretence: Gules a fess vair between three molets argent (Baugh), impaling, Azure semy-de-lis a lion rampant argent langued gules (Holland)
Viscountess's coronet   Supporters: Two mermaids holding looking-glasses proper
For Harriet, only dau. of Benjamin Baugh, of Burwarton House, who m. 1796, Gustavus, 6th Viscount Boyne, and d. 1 Nov. 1854.   (B.P. 1949 ed.)

2. All black background
Arms: As 1.
Viscount's coronet   Crest: From a ducal coronet or an oak tree traversed by a framesaw proper   Motto: Nec timeo nec sperno
Supporters: As 1.
For Gustavus, 6th Viscount Boyne, d. 1 Nov. 1854.   (B.P. 1949 ed.)

DORRINGTON

1. All black background
Azure a chevron or between three bezants (Hope)   In pretence: Gules

a chevron ermine between three tigers' heads erased argent (Edwardes)
Crest: A globe azure surmounted by a rainbow with clouds at each end proper   Mantling: Gules and argent   Motto: In coelo quies
For John Thomas Hope, who m. 1794, Ellen Hester Mary, only child and heir of Sir Thomas Edwardes, 6th Bt., and d. 13 Mar. 1854.   (B.L.G. 1937 ed.)

2. Dexter background black
Qly, 1st and 4th, Gules a chevron ermine between three griffins' heads argent (Edwardes), 2nd and 3rd, Azure two chevronels or between four bezants two and one (Hope), impaling, Qly per fess indented or and gules (Leighton)
Crests: Dexter, A Saracen's head facing to the dexter proper   Sinister, As 1., but with a palm branch on each side of the globe proper
Mantling: Gules and argent   Mottoes: Gratia naturam vincit   Yet I have hope
For Thomas Henry Hope-Edwardes, who m. 1833, Louisa Charlotte, eldest dau. of Col. Francis Knyvett Leighton, of Bausley, and d. 6 Apr. 1871. (B.L.G. 1937 ed.)

EATON-UNDER-HAYWOOD

1. All black background
Qly, 1st, Qly azure and or four lions rampant counterchanged (Lutley), 2nd, qly i. & iv. Argent in chief three ravens sable, (Corbin), ii. & iii. Argent in chief a lion passant gules in base three leopards' faces sable (Filiode), 3rd, Azure a cinquefoil and a bordure ermine (Astley), 4th, Argent three boars' heads sable langued gules a chief indented sable (Jenkes)
Crest: (torn away)   Mantling: Gules and argent   Motto: Virtute non vi
Probably for Jenks Lutley, b. 1710 and d. unm., the eldest son of Philip Lutley of Lawton, and Penelope, née Barneby.   (B.L.G. 1937 ed.)
(This hatchment was recorded in 1962 and reported as missing in 1979.)

EDGMOND

1. All black background
Argent a fess azure between three cocks' heads erased sable combed and wattled gules, on a bordure gules nine crowns or (Alcock)
Crest: A cock proper   Mantling: Gules and azure
Unidentified

EDGTON

1. Dexter background black
Per chevron sable and ermine in chief two boars' heads couped close or (Sandford), impaling, Gules three chevronels argent (Jones)

Crest: A boar's head proper in its mouth a pheon or   Mantling: Gules and argent   Motto: Mors janua vitæ
For Humphrey Sandford, who m. 1746, Elizabeth, only child of Hugh Jones, and d. 31 July 1791.   (B.L.G. 1937 ed.)

2. All black background
Qly, 1st, Per chevron sable and ermine in chief two boars' heads proper (Sandford), 2nd, Per fess gules and vert a fess and in chief a chevron argent (Springseaux), 3rd, Gules three chevronels argent (Jones), 4th, Argent on a bend vert three nags' heads erased argent (Middleton)   In pretence: Azure semy-de-lis a lion rampant guardant argent (Holland)
Crest: A boar's head proper in its mouth a pheon or   Mantling: Gules and argent   Motto: Nec timere nec timide
For the Rev. Humphrey Sandford, who m. 1811, Frances only child of the Rev. George Holland, and d. 13 Sept. 1856.   (B.L.G. 1937 ed.)

FRODESLEY

1. Dexter background black
Qly of twelve, 1st and 12th, Gules a chevron between three tigers' heads erased argent (Edwardes), 2nd, Per bend sinister ermine and sable ermined argent a lion rampant or (Tudor Trevor), 3rd, Argent a chevron gules between three roundels azure (Baskerville), 4th, Or two bars gules, on a chief azure an escutcheon ermine (   ), 5th, Chequy argent and sable (   ), 6th, Argent a chevron between three shelducks ? sable (   ), 7th, Or a chevron between three leopards' faces gules (   ), 8th, Or three chessrooks and a chief embattled sable (Rocke), 9th, Qly per fess indented ermine and azure (   ), 10th, Sable three ears of corn ? argent (   ), 11th, Azure a chevron or between three bezants (Hope), at fess point the Badge of Ulster, impaling, Hope
Crest: A man's head and shoulders affronté in armour the vizor open proper   Mantling: Gules and argent   Motto: Gratia natural vincit
For Sir Henry Edwardes, 9th Bt., who m. 1828, Louisa Mary, dau. of John Thomas Hope, of Netley Hall, and d. 2 Aug. 1841.   (B.P. 1878 ed.)

HALSTON Hall Chapel (nr Oswestry)
(This private Chapel is not open to the public)

1. Sinister background black
Argent a cinquefoil azure (Mytton), impaling, Argent from a mount sable three hop-poles sustaining their fruit all proper (Houblon)
Crest: A ram's head argent horned or   Mantling: Gules and argent   Motto: Mors iter ad vita

For Arabella, dau. of Sir John Houblon, Kt., who m. Richard Mytton of Halsted (living 1690). (B.L.G. 1853 ed.)

2. Dexter background black
Mytton   In pretence: Argent a lion rampant and a canton sable (Owen)
Crest: A bull's head couped sable charged with three annulets or
Mantling: As 1.   Motto: Mors iter ad vitam
For Richard Mytton, who m. Letitia, dau. and eventual heiress of Roger Owen of Condover, and d. 27 Feb. 1730/1.   (Source, as 1.)

3. Dexter background black
Mytton, impaling, A chevron sable between three cross crosslets fitchy sable (Davenport)
Crest and mantling: As 1.   Motto: indecipherable
For John Mytton, who m. Mary Elizabeth, dau. of Henry Davenport of Davenport House, and d. 1756.   (Source, as 1.)

4. Dexter background black
Mytton, impaling, Ermine three fusils conjoined in fess sable (Pigott)
Crest and mantling: As 1.   Motto: Mors iter vita
For John Mytton, who m. Rebecca, dau. of Robert Pigott, of Chetwynd, and d. 26 Oct. 1783.   (Source, as 1.)

5. All black background
On a lozenge   Arms: As 4.
For Rebecca, widow of John Mytton

6. Dexter background black
Mytton, impaling, Owen
Crest: A ram's head argent   Mantling: As 1.   Motto: In coelo quies
For John Mytton, who m. Harriett, dau. of William Mostyn Owen, of Woodhouse, and d. 1826.   (Source, as 1.)

7. Sinister background black
Qly, 1st and 4th, Per pale azure and gules a double-headed eagle displayed or within a bordure engrailed or (Mytton), 2nd and 3rd, Argent a cinquefoil azure (Mytton), impaling, Argent a lion rampant sable (for Jones)
Motto: In coelo quies
For Harriett, dau. of Sir Thomas Tyrwhitt Jones, who m. as his first wife, John Mytton, and d. 2 July 1820.   (Source, as 1.)

HARLEY

1. Dexter background black
Per pale in chief and per fess, 1st, Argent six roundels three, two and one gules (Harnage), 2nd, Argent a lion rampant and in chief three roundels

gules (Harnage), 3rd, Argent two bars sable each charged with three
escallops or (Shenton), impaling, Argent a cross sable (Rainsford)
Crest: From a ducal coronet or a lion's gamb proper holding a roundel
gules   Mantling: Gules and argent   Motto: Deo duce decrevi
Two cherubs' heads in base
For William Henry Harnage, who m. 1792, Mary, dau. and co-heir of
Henry Rainsford, of Much Wenlock, and d.s.p. 15 July 1820.   (B.P.
1875 ed.)

2. All black background
Qly, 1st and 4th, Harnage, 2nd and 3rd, Sable ermined argent three lions
rampant or, a bordure or charged with crescents azure (Blackman), over
all the Badge of Ulster, impaling, Azure crusilly a lion rampant argent
(Goodrich)
Crest, mantling and motto: As 1.
For Sir George Harnage, 2nd Bt., who m. 1826, Caroline Helena, youngest dau. and co-heir of Bartlett Goodrich, of Saling Grove, Essex, and
d. 10 Mar. 1866.   (B.P. 1875 ed.)

HOPTON WAFERS

1. Dexter background black
Barry of twelve sable and or (Botfield), impaling, Azure on a cross
between four garbs or an escallop between four ermine spots sable
(Skelhorne)
Crest: A reindeer statant or   Mantling: Gules and argent   Motto:
J'ay bonne cause
For Thomas Botfield, of Hopton Court, who m. 1800, Lucy, dau. of
William Skelhorne, of Liverpool, and d. 17 Jan. 1843.   (B.L.G. 2nd
ed.; M.I.)

LEATON

1. All black background
Qly of nine, 1st, Per bend sinister ermine and ermines a lion rampant or
a bordure gules (Lloyd), 2nd, Azure three crowns or (   ), 3rd, Azure a
lion rampant argent on a bordure argent nine roundels sable (   ), 4th,
Ermine a lion rampant sable (   ), 5th, Azure three boars in pale
argent a bordure engrailed or (   ), 6th, Per bend sinister ermine and
sable ermined argent a lion rampant or (Lloyd), 7th, Azure three geese
argent (   ), 8th, Or on a chief sable three escallops or, a bordure
sable (Graham), 9th, Gules a lion rampant or, on a chief argent a crescent
between two molets azure (Ligonier)
Crest: A demi-lion rampant or   Mantling: Gules and argent   Motto:
Retinens vestigia famæ
Possibly for John Arthur Lloyd, who d. unm. 22 June 1864.   (B.L.G.
1871 ed.; M.I.)

2. All black background
Arms: As 1.
Crest, mantling and motto: As 1.
Cherub's head in base
Possibly for Charles Spencer Lloyd, who d. 20 June 1876.   (B.L.G. 1937 ed.; M.I.)

LEIGHTON

1. All black background
Azure crusilly a lion rampant argent (Kynnersley), impaling, Or a fret azure (Eyton)
Crest: A greyhound sejant argent collared or beneath a hawthorn tree fructed proper   Mantling: Gules and argent   Motto: In coelo quies
For Thomas Kynnersley, who m. Anne, dau. of Thomas Eyton, and d. 15 Apr. 1843.   (B.L.G. 5th ed.; M.I.)

LINLEY

1. All black background
Quarterly per fess A ermine and azure (Lacon), impaling,   Argent two bends azure, on a canton azure a cinqefoil or (Pippard)
Crest: A falcon belled or   Mantling: Gules and argent   Motto: In caelo quies
For Richard Lacon, who m. Mary, dau. of Henry Pippard, and d. 1803. (B.L.G. 1853 ed.)

LLAN-Y-BLODWELL

1. All black background
Qly of eighteen, 1st, Gules a double-headed eagle displayed between three fleurs-de-lis argent (Godolphin), 2nd, Per fess sable and argent a lion/wolf counterchanged, on a canton argent a castle gules (   ), 3rd, Argent a chevron gules between three pheons the two in chief pointing to the centre sable (Cadwgan), 4th, Per pale azure and sable three fleurs-de-lis or (   ), 5th, 12th and 16th, Sable three horses' heads erased argent (   ), 6th and 15th, Ermine a lion rampant sable (   ), 7th, Argent a lion rampant sable crowned or (Owen), 8th, Or a lion rampant gules (   ), 9th, Per bend sinister ermine and sable ermined argent a lion rampant or (   ), 10th, Ermine a lion rampant azure (   ), 11th, Gules three chevrons argent (   ), 13th, Argent a lion rampant sable (   ), 14th, Sable a lion rampant or (   ), 17th, Azure two bars gemel and in chief a lion passant regardant or (Tregoz), 18th, as 1st
On a lozenge surrounded by floriated scroll work
Unidentified

LONGNOR

1. All black background
Or two ravens in pale proper within a bordure engrailed gules bezanty, in

Shropshire

chief the Badge of Ulster (Corbett)
Crest: A raven, in its beak a sprig of holly fructed proper   Mantling: Gules and argent   Motto: Deus pascit corvos
For Sir Richard Corbett, 4th Bt., M.P. for Shrewsbury, b. 1696, d. unm, 25 Sept. 1774.   (B.E.B.)

2. Dexter background black
Or two ravens in pale proper within a bordure engrailed gules bezanty (Corbett), impaling to the dexter, Argent on a chevron between three cross crosslets fitchy sable an escallop argent (Russell), and to the sinister, Gules a chevron vair between three talbots' heads erased or (Isted) Crest, mantling and motto: As 1.
For Robert Corbett (formerly Flint), who m. 2nd, Anne, dau. of Ambrose Isted, and d.   She d. 1822.   (B.L.G. 1853 ed.)

3. All black background
Qly, 1st, Corbett, 2nd, Per fess azure and or in base a mascle gules (Plymley), 3rd, Or on a chevron gules three bars sable (Proud), 4th, Azure a pale or (   )   To dexter of main shield, qly as above, impaling, Gules two bars ermine, on a canton sable a millrind argent (Panton) S.B1. To sinister of main shield, Qly as above, impaling, Barry wavy of six argent and gules (Dansey) S.B1.
Crest, mantling and motto: As 1.
For the Rev. Joseph Plymley, Archdeacon of Salop, who assumed the surname and arms of Corbett. He m. 1st, Jane Josepha, dau. of Thomas Panton, and 2nd, Matty, 3rd dau. of Dansey Dansey, of Brinsop, co. Hereford, and d. 22 June 1830, aged 79.   (B.L.G. 1937 ed.)

4. Dexter background black
Qly, 1st, Corbett, 2nd, Plymley, 3rd, Proud, 4th, Gules two bars sable ermined argent, on a canton azure a chessrook argent, a crescent for difference (Panton), impaling, Qly, 1st and 4th, Azure three cocks argent (for Jones), 2nd and 3rd, Gules three serpents intertwined or (   )
Crest, mantling and motto: As 1.
For Panton Corbett, who m. 1814, Lucy Favoreeta, dau. of Dr. Jones, of Lichfield, and d. Nov. 1855.   (B.L.G. 1937 ed.)

5. All black background
On a lozenge surmounted by an urn with a cherub's head in each angle, Azure a cross engrailed or between four roses argent seeded or (Burton), impaling, Corbett
For Ellen, dau. of the Rev. Joseph Corbett, D.D., of Longnor, who m. 1825, Edward Burton, and d.   (B.L.G. 1937 ed.)

LOPPINGTON

1. All black background
Argent three boars' heads couped sable a crescent gules for difference
(   ), impaling, Argent a lion rampant and a canton sable (Owen)
Crest: indistinguishable   Mantling: Gules and argent   On motto
scroll: Anno Dom. 1694   Skull in base
Unidentified

2. All black background
On a lozenge   Sable three bowls or issuant from each a boar's head
couped argent (Bolas), impaling, Azure an arm in armour embowed
proper issuing from the sinister holding a rose gules slipped and leaved
proper (Chambre)
On motto scroll: Mrs. Katherine Bolas, died 1756
For Katherine, dau. of Arthur Chambre, who m. Roger Bolas, of Ryton,
and bur. 17 Sept. 1756.   (B.L.G. 2nd ed.; inscr. on hatchment; M.I.)

3. Dexter background black
Qly, 1st and 4th, Azure three lions rampant or (Noneley), 2nd and 3rd,
Argent two marigolds in fess gules slipped and leaved proper (Marigold)
Crest: A lion rampant or   Mantling: Gules and argent   Motto:
Resurgemus   Winged skull in base
Probably for Thomas Noneley, son of Richard Noneley and Margaret
(neé Marigold), who d. 5 July 1799.   (M.I.)

4. All black background
Argent a chevron between three cross crosslets fitchy sable (   ),
impaling, Azure three lions rampant or (Nonely)
Crest: A lion rampant argent   Mantling: Gules and argent
Motto: In coelo quies   Skull in base
Unidentified

LUDFORD

1. All black background
Qly, 1st and 4th, Sable a chevron between three storks' heads erased
argent (Waring), 2nd, Sable a chevron between three owls affronté argent
(Broughton), 3rd, Argent on a fess sable three   or (   ), impaling,
Qly, 1st, Qly argent and gules a fret or over all a fess azure (Norreys),
2nd, Azure a chief argent (   ), 3rd, Azure a cross moline
surmounted by a ducal coronet or (   ), 4th, Argent on a rock an
eagle rising sable (   )
Crest: A demi-heron or winged argent   Mantling: Gules and argent
Unidentified

LYDBURY NORTH

1. Sinister background black
Argent on a fess sable three molets or (Clive)   In pretence: Per pale azure and gules three lions rampant argent (Herbert)
On a shield surmounted by an earl's coronet
For Henrietta Antonia, dau. of Henry Arthur Herbert Powis, who m. Edward, 1st Earl of Powis, and d. 3 June 1830.   (B.P. 1939 ed.)

2. All black background
Arms: As 1.   Earl's coronet
Crest: A griffin passant argent   Mantling: Gules and argent
Motto: Resurgam   Supporters: Dexter, An elephant argent Sinister, A griffin wings expanded argent, charged with three molets or
For Edward, 1st Earl of Powis, who d. 16 May 1839.   (B.P. 1939 ed.)

LYDHAM

1. All black background
Argent on a fess between three crescents gules three fleurs-de-lis or (Oakeley), impaling, Per pale, dexter, Gules a lion rampant reguardant or, sinister, Argent three boars' heads couped close sable (Lloyd)
Crest: A dexter arm in armour embowed holding a dagger proper
Mantling: Gules and argent   Motto: Resurgam
For William Oakeley, of Oakeley, who m. 1834, Alice Mary, dau. of Gen. Sir Evan Lloyd, of Ferney Hall, Salop, and d.s.p. June 1851. (B.L.G. 5th ed.)

MORE

1. All black background
Sable a swan proper a bordure engrailed or (More)
Crests: Dexter, An eagle proper preying on a coney argent   Sinister, From a ducal coronet or a swan's neck proper   Mantling: Gules and argent   Motto: Memento mori
For Thomas More, of More, who d. 1731.   Or for Rev. Robert Henry More, d. May 1879.   (B.L.G. 1937 ed.)

2. All black background
Per pale azure a gules a double-headed eagle displayed within a bordure engrailed or (Mytton)
Crest: A bull's head couped proper charged with three bezants
Mantling: Gules and argent
Probably for Thomas Mytton, of Cleobury North, d. unm. 2 Mar. 1818. (B.L.G. 7th ed.)

MORVILLE

1. All black background
Gules a cross engrailed argent in the first quarter a lozenge or (Leigh)   In pretence: Per pale or and gules two lions rampant addorsed counterchanged (Blayney for Weaver)
Viscount's coronet   Crest: A celestial crown proper   Mantling: Gules and argent   Motto: Resurgam   Winged skulls and crossbones on frame
For Henry, 8th Viscount Tracy, who assumed the name and arms of Leigh by Royal Licence in 1793, m. Susannah, dau. of Anthony Weaver, of Morville, and heiress of her cousin Arthur Blayney, and d. 27 Apr. 1797   (G.E.C.)

2. All black background
Sable a bend between six martlets argent (Smyth), impaling to the dexter, Per pale or and gules two lions rampant addorsed counterchanged (Blayney), and to the sinister, Argent three bars gemel sable (   )   Also, in pretence: Qly, 1st and 4th, Gules a lion rampant reguardant or, 2nd and 3rd, Argent three boars' heads couped sable (Lloyd of Ferney Hall)
Crest: A lion's gamb erased erect proper   Mantling: Gules and argent
Motto: Mors janua vitæ   Skull and crossbones in base
Unidentified

MYDDLE

1. All black background
Azure two lions rampant gules supporting a garb or (Hanmer), impaling, Argent on a chevron gules five pears or, in base a Catherine wheel sable (   )
Crest: A lion rampant gules   Mantling: Gules and argent
For Edward Hanmer, of Marton, who d. 20 Apr. 1770.   (M.I.)

2. Dexter background black
Gules on a fess engrailed argent between three griffins' heads erased or three crosses formy fitchy sable (Atcherley), impaling, Argent a fess sable ermined argent cotised sable between three ravens proper (Edwards)
Crest: A demi-bustard gules winged or in its beak a lily proper
Mantling: Gules and argent   Motto: Resurgam
For Richard Atcherley, who m. Elizabeth, dau. of Arthur Edwards, and d. 27 Feb. 1834.   (B.L.G. 5th ed.)
(This hatchment, originally recorded in 1953, is now missing)

3. Dexter background black
Atcherley   In pretence: Qly, 1st and 4th, Argent a chevron between three griffins' heads erased sable (Topping?), 2nd and 3rd, Vert a fess between three bucks or (Robinson)
Crest and mantling: As 2.   Motto: Spes mea in Deo
For David Francis Atcherley, of Myddle, who m. 1817, Anne Margaret, dau. of James Topping, by Sarah Margaret, dau. and heiress of William Robinson, and d. 1845.   (B.L.G. 5th ed.)

Shropshire

NASH

1. Dexter background black
Ermine on a fess sable a castle triple-towered argent (Hill), impaling, Or a lion's gamb in bend gules in sinister chief a cross crosslet fitchy gules (for Powys)
Crest: Indecipherable   Mantling: Gules and argent
For Andrew Hill, who m. Anne, dau. of Thomas Powys, of Henley, Salop, and d. 23 Aug. 1708.   (B.L.G. 1853 ed.)

2. All black background
Hill arms as 1.
Crest: A tower argent   Mantling: Gules and argent   Motto: In Coelo Quies
Unidentified

3. Dexter background black
Or on a bend cotised sable three wolves' heads erased or (Lowe)   In pretence Hill
Crest: A demi-lion rampant or   Mantling: Gules and argent   Motto: Meliora spero
For Thomas Lowe, first husband of Lucy, dau. and co-heiress of Thomas Hill, who d. 10 Nov. 1797.   (Source, as 1.)

4. Dexter background black
Qly, 1st and 4th, Or three crescents azure on a canton sable a crown or (Hodges), 2nd and 3rd, Argent a fret gules (   ), impaling, Azure on a chevron between three lions passant guardant or three crosses moline sable (Fowler)   In pretence, Hill
Crest: Dexter, Out of a ducal coronet sable?   Sinister, A crowned angel
Mantling: Gules and argent   Motto: In coelo quies
For Thomas Hodges, son of Col. Hodges and his wife, Sarah dau. of Sir Richard Fowler, 2nd Bt. Mr. Hodges assumed the name of Fowler and m. Lucy Hill, (as her second husband), and d. 6 June 1820.   (Sources, as 1; Burke's Extinct Bts. sub Fowler)
(These hatchments were in poor condition when recorded and have since been restored by the National Trust at Attingham Park)

GREAT NESS

1. All black background
Per fess sable and argent a lion rampant counterchanged (Edwards), impaling, Argent a chevron gules between three talbots sable on a canton gules the legs of Man argent (for Martin)
Crest: A lion rampant per fess argent and sable within a wreath argent and sable   Mantling: Gules and argent   Motto: In coelo quies   Cherub's head in base
For John Edwards, who d. 1850. He m. Charlotte, dau. of the Rev. George Martin, and Lady Mary Murray (dau. of John, 3rd Duke of Atholl). (B.L.G. 1853 ed.)

NEWPORT
1. All black background
Qly, 1st and 4th, Argent a cross wavy, in the first quarter an eagle wings displayed sable (Webb), 2nd and 3rd, Sable a stag couchant argent (Downes)   In pretence: Qly, 1st and 4th, Paly of six argent and azure a millrind sable (Mills), 2nd and 3rd, Argent a bend engrailed gules a chief indented vert (   )
Crest: A demi-eagle argent langued and ducally gorged gules
Mantling: Gules and argent
Unidentified

NORTON-IN-HALES
1. All black backgrond
Qly, 1st and 4th, Sable a griffin segreant argent (Griffin), 2nd and 3rd, Gules a cross flory or (Latimer)
Crest: A talbot's head proper   Mantling: Gules and argent   Motto: In coelo quies   Winged skull in base
For Alfred William Griffin, of Brand Hall, who d. unm. 18 Dec. 1861. (B.L.G. 1937 ed.)

PITCHFORD
1. All black background
Argent on a bend azure three oat-sheaves or (Ottley)
Crest: An oat-sheaf or   Mantling: Gules and argent   Motto: Oblier ne Doy   Winged skull in base
Probably for Adam Ottley, who d. 1807.   (The General Armoury)

2. Sinister background black
Ottley   In pretence: Azure on a fess wavy argent a cross formy gules in chief two estoiles or (Jenkinson)
Motto: As 1.   Winged skull below   A very small hatchment, c. 18 ins x 18 ins
For Catherine, dau. of Sir Banks Jenkinson, Bt., who m. Ottley, Esq., and mother of No 1. She died Dec. 1792.

3. Sinister background black
Azure a fess between three estoiles argent (Jenkinson)   In pretence: Qly, 1st and 4th, Azure a griffin passant and a chief or (Evelyn), 2nd and 3rd, Sable a chevron between three molets argent (Shuckburgh)
Motto: Pareo no servio
For Julia Evelyn Medley, dau. of Sir George Shuckburgh-Evelyn, who m. Charles Cecil Cope Jenkinson, later 3rd Earl of Liverpool, and d. 8 Apr. 1814.   (B.E.P.)

4. All black background
Azure a fess wavy argent charged with a cross formy gules in chief two estoiles argent, on a chief wavy argent a cormorant in the beak a branch of laver proper, in dexter chief the Badge of Ulster (Jenkinson),

Earl's coronet
Crest: A sea horse or maned sable holding a cross formy gules   Motto: Palma non sine pulvere   Supporters: Two hawks proper belled or charged on their breasts with a cross formy gules
Probably for Charles, 3rd Earl of Liverpool, who d. 6 Mar. 1855.
(B.E.P.)

5. Dexter background black
Qly ermine and paly of six or and gules (Cotes)   In pretence: Qly, 1st, Azure a fess wavy argent charged with a cross formy gules in chief two estoiles argent (Jenkinson), 2nd, Shuckburgh, 3rd, Azure a griffin passant or a chief argent (Evelyn), 4th, Sable two bars gemel on a chief argent three molets sable (Medley)
Crest: A cock gules   Mantling: Gules and argent   Motto: Soli Deo honor et gloria
For John Cotes, of Woodcote Hall, who m. 1839, Louisa Harriet, dau. of Charles, 3rd Earl of Liverpool, and d. 1874. She d. 5 Feb. 1887.
(B.L.G. 1937 ed.; B.E.P)

6. All black background
Two shields accolé   Dexter, Qly, 1st and 4th, Gules on a fess engrailed between three antique crowns or a lion passant guardant between two cinquefoils gules (Grant), 2nd, Coates, 3rd, Jenkinson as 4 with estoiles or all within the Order of the Bath   Sinister, Qly, 1st and 4th, Vert three primroses within a double tressure flory-counter-flory or (Primrose), 2nd and 3rd, Argent a lion rampant double queued sable (Cressy),
Suspended below are the badges of the Order of the Bath, The Royal Victoria Order and the Distinguised Service Order.
Knight's helm   Crest: A burning hill proper   Mantling: Or and gules   Motto: (above crest) Stand Fast
For Gen. Sir Charles John Cecil Grant, of Sheuglie, K.C.B., K.C.V.O., D.S.O., who m. Lady Sybil Myra Caroline Primrose, dau. of the 5th Earl of Rosebery, and d. 9 Nov. 1950.   (family)

7. All black background
Arms as dexter of 6.
Crests: Dexter as 6,   Sinister, A cock ermine winged paly or and gules   Mantling: Dexter, or and gules   Sinister, argent and sable
Mottoes: (above dexter crest) Standing fast   (above sinister crest) Soli Deo honor et gloria
For Charles Robert Archibald Grant, son of No 6, who d. 21 Jan. 1972 (Source, as 6)

QUATT

1. All black background
Vert fretty or (Whitmore), impaling, Sable ten roundels four, three, two and one argent, on a chief argent a lion passant sable, langued gules

(Bridgeman)
Crest: On the stump of a tree a falcon proper beaked and belled or
Mantling: Gules and argent   Motto: Dormiens in Jesu
For William Wolryche-Whitmore, who m. 1810, Lucy Elizabeth
Georgiana, dau. of Orlando, 1st Earl of Bradford, and d. 1858.
(B.L.G. 1937 ed.)
(This hatchment has been restored recently, 1990)

RUYTON-OF-THE-XI-TOWNS

1. All black background
On a lozenge surmounted by a cherub's head
Argent a lion rampant sable (Kynaston)   In pretence: Argent a lion rampant sable (Kynaston)
Winged skull below
For Margaret, youngest daughter of William Kynaston, who m. Edward Kynaston (d. 1792) and d. 1806, aged 76.   (M.I.)

2. All black background
On an ornate shield, intended for a lozenge, surmounted by an urn, and with a cherub's head in each other angle
Qly, 1st and 4th, Argent a lion rampant sable (Kynaston), 2nd and 3rd, qly i. & iv. Argent a lion rampant sable (Kynaston), ii. & iii. Gules three roses or barbed and seeded proper, a chief chequy argent and sable (Taylor)
For either Margaret, d. 12 Sept. 1845, or Anne, d. 8 Oct. 1838, daughters of Edward and Margaret Kynaston.   (M.I.)

3. All black background
On a lozenge surmounted by an urn, flanked by cherubs' heads and with another in base
Qly, 1st and 4th, Argent on a bend vert three greyhounds' heads erased argent (Middelton), 2nd, Per pale gules and azure three saltires argent (Lane), 3rd, Argent a lion rampant sable (Kynaston)
Inscribed on frame: Anna Maria Middelton, d. 27 Jan. 1851. Buried at Great Comberton, Worcs.

4. All black background
On a roughly lozenge shaped shield, surmounted by an urn, and flanked by cherubs' heads
Azure a lion rampant guardant within an orle of eight fleurs-de-lis argent (Holland)
For Martha Holland, dau. of Thomas and Jane Holland, of Teyrden, Denbighshire, d. 1756.   (M.I.)

ST MARTIN'S

1. All black background (actually yellowish-green)
Qly, 1st and 4th, Per bend sinister ermine and sable ermined argent a lion

rampant or (Trevor), 2nd and 3rd, Sable on a fess argent between three lions passant or three escallops gules (Hill), impaling, Argent on a bend azure three popinjays or (Curzon)
Baron's coronet   Crest: Dexter, A wyvern sable with motto, Quid verum atque decens, above   Sinister, A stag's head proper collared and attired or, with motto, Per Deum et ferrum obtinui, above   Supporters: Dexter, A lion sable ermined argent ducally gorged and chained or, dependent from the coronet a shield, Argent a wyvern sable   Sinister, A hound proper, spotted, collared and chained or, dependent from the coronet a shield, Ermine a stag's head proper attired or
For Arthur Edwin, 1st Baron Trevor, who m. 2nd, 1858, Mary Catherine Curzon (d. 20 Aug. 1911), and d. 25 Dec. 1894.   (B.P. 1939 ed.)

2. Dexter background black
Qly, 1st and 4th, Trevor, 2nd and 3rd, Hill, impaling, Qly, 1st and 4th, Argent three holy leaves proper (Irvine), 2nd and 3rd, Azure three cinquefoils between nine cross crosslets argent (D'Arcy)
Viscount's coronet   Crest: On a chapeau gules and ermine a wyvern sable   Motto: Quid verum atque decens   Supporters: Two lions or ermined sable
For Arthur, 3rd Viscount Dungannon, who m. 1821, Sophia (d. 21 Mar. 1880), dau. of Col. Gorges Marcus D'Arcy Irvine, of Castle Irvine, co. Fermanagh, and d.s.p. 11 Aug. 1862.   (B.P. 1965 ed.)
(This hatchment, recorded in May, 1955, is now missing)

SHIFNAL

1. All black background
On a wood panel
Qly of six, 1st, 3rd, and 5th, Argent a chevron between three trefoils slipped sable (Moreton), 2nd, 4th, and 6th, Gules a cockerel statant or (Hamer)
Crest: A cock's head or wings expanded azure collared with a fess doubly cotised gules, combed or, in the beak a trefoil slipped sable   Mantling: Gules and argent
Unidentified

SHIPTON

1. All black background
Sable a swan close argent beaked and legged or a bordure engrailed or (More), impaling, Per pale azure and gules a double-headed eagle displayed within a bordure engrailed or (Mytton)
Crest: An eagle preying on a coney proper   Mantling: Gules and argent   Motto: Memento mori
For Thomas More, of Larden Hall, who m. 1795, Harriott, dau. of Thomas Mytton, of Shipton, and d. 13 June 1804.   (B.L.G. 1937 ed.)

2. All black background
Mytton arms only
Crest: A bull's head erased sable bezanty armed argent   Mantling: Gules and argent
Unidentified
(This hatchment is now missing)

SHREWSBURY, New St Chad's
1. Sinister background black
Qly per fess indented or and gules, a crescent gules for difference (Leighton)   In pretence: Gules a lion rampant or between three escallops argent, on a chief argent three pellets engrailed azure (Adams)
Cherub's head above
For Clare, sister and co-heir of John Boynton Adams, who m. the Rev. Francis Leighton, as his 1st wife, and d. 1801.   (B.P. 1949 ed.)

2. Dexter background black
Leighton, as 1.   In pretence: Adams, as 1. Also impaling, Qly per fess indented or and gules (Leighton)
Crest: A wyvern wings endorsed sable   Mantling: Gules and argent
Motto: Mors janua vitæ   Cherub's head below
For the Rev. Francis Leighton, who m. 1st, Clare, sister and co-heir of John Boynton Adams, and 2nd, Victoria, dau. of Baldwin Leighton, and d. 1813.   (B.P. 1949 ed.)

3. Dexter background black
Qly, 1st and 4th, Leighton, as 1. but no crescent in 4th quarter, 2nd, Azure a chevron between three fleurs-de-lis ermine (Burgh), 3rd, Adams, as 1., impaling,   Azure fretty argent a chief or (St Leger)
Crest: A wyvern wings expanded sable   Mantling: Gules and argent
Motto: Dread shame
For Francis Knyvett Leighton, who m. Louisa Ann, dau. of St Leger, 1st Viscount Doneraile, and d. 19 Nov. 1834.   (B.P. 1949 ed.)

4. All black background
On a lozenge-shaped shield, surmounted by an urn
Arms: As 3., but chevron argent in 2nd quarter
Shield flanked by palm branches and two cherub's heads
For Louisa Ann, widow of No. 3, who d. 1834.   (B.P. 1949 ed.)

5. All black background
Argent three catherine wheels sable within a bordure engrailed gules (Scott)
Crest: A demi-griffin segreant sable beaked and membered or
Mantling: Gules and argent   Motto: In coelo quies
Probably for Richard Scott, who d. unm. 29 Apr. 1821.   (B.L.G. 5th ed.; Scott family papers)

6. Dexter background black
Scott, impaling, Argent a battleaxe in pale gules between three roundels azure (Morse)
Crest and mantling: As 5.   Motto: Recte faciendo neminem timeas
For George John Scott, of Betton, who m. 1802, Anne, dau. of William Morse, of Ealing, and d. 29 May 1811.   (Sources, as 5.)

7. All black background
On an elaborately decorated lozenge surmounted by an antique crown, Scott   In pretence: Argent three cocks gules (Cockburne)
A cherub's head on either side of lozenge
For Lucretia, dau. of Charles Cockburne, who m. the Rev. George Scott, of Betton, and d. 18 July 1832. He d. 25 Oct. 1799.   (Sources, as 5.)

8. All black background
Qly, 1st and 4th, Scott, 2nd and 3rd, Cockburne, at fess point a crescent for difference
Crest, mantling and motto: As 7.
For Richard Scott, B.D., son of the Rev. George Scott and Lucretia Cockburne, who d. 6 Oct. 1848   (Sources, as 5.)

9. Dexter background black
Or three chessrooks and a chief embattled sable (Rocke), impaling, Sable three lions' heads erased argent crowned or (Kinchant)
Crest: On a rock proper a martlet or   Mantling: Gules and argent
Motto: In Deo spes est nostra   Skull in base
For Richard Rocke, who m. Eliza, dau. of Capt. John Kinchant, and d.   (B.L.G. 1937 ed.)

10. Dexter background black
Rocke, impaling, Qly, 1st and 4th, Argent a lion rampant sable armed and langued gules (Owen), 2nd and 3rd, Argent a cross floretty engrailed sable between four choughs proper, on a chief azure a boar's head couped close argent (Owen)
Crest and mantling: As 9.   Motto: Si Deus pro nobis quis contra nos
For the Rev. John Rocke, who m. 1782, Harriet (d. 14 May 1831), dau. of the Rev. Pryce Owen, and d. 4 June 1824.   (B.L.G. 1937 ed.)

11. All black background
Qly, 1st and 4th, Gules a chevron engrailed between three wolves' heads erased argent, a crescent gules for difference (Edwardes), 2nd, Per bend sinister ermine and sable ermined argent a lion rampant or (Tudor Trevor), 3rd, Argent a chevron gules between three roundels vert (Baskerville)   In pretence: Qly, 1st, Vert three eagles rising argent (Smitheman), 2nd, Chequy argent and sable (Brooke), 3rd, Gules a talbot passant argent (   ), 4th, Vert semy-de-lis a lion rampant or (   )
Crest: A man's head in a helmet affronté proper   Mantling: Gules and

argent   Motto: A vyno Duw dervid
For Major Benjamin Edwardes, who m. Catherine, eldest dau. of John Smitheman, and d.   (B.P. 1875 ed.)

12. All black background
Qly, 1st and 4th, Edwardes, as 11., 2nd and 3rd, Vert three eagles rising argent collared or (Smitheman)
Crest, mantling and motto: As 11.
For John Thomas Smitheman Edwardes, who d. 31 Oct. 1851.   (B.P. 1875 ed.)

13. All black background
Argent on a bend gules cotised sable three pairs of wings conjoined in lure argent (Wingfield), impaling, Ermine two chevrons azure (Bagot)
Crest: A high bonnet per pale argent and sable banded gules between two wings displayed counterchanged, the sable throughout gutté d'argent
Mantling: Gules and argent   Motto: In coelo quies
For Rowland Wingfield, who m. 1764, Mary, dau. of Sir Walter Bagot, Bt., of Blithfield, Staffs., and d. 10 Aug. 1818, aged 90.   (B.L.G. 5th ed.)

14. All black background
Wingfield, impaling, Or three chessrooks and a chief embattled sable (Rocke)
Crest: As 13., but tinctures reversed   Mantling and motto: As 13.
Cherub's head in base
For John Wingfield, of Onslow, who m. 1811, Mary Anne, only dau. of the Rev. John Rocke, of Shrewsbury, and d. 31 Aug. 1862.   (B.L.G. 5th ed.)

15. All black background
Per fess gules and argent three cinquefoils counterchanged (Swinburne)
In pretence: Azure a chevron ermine between three spears or (Spearman)
Crest: From a ducal coronet or a demi-boar rampant argent   Mantling: Gules and argent   Motto: Semel et semper
For Thomas Swinburne, of Pontop Hall, who m. 1781, Charlotte, dau. and co-heir of Robert Spearman, and d. Oct. 1825.   (B.P. 1949 ed.)

16. All black background
On an ornate lozenge-shaped shield, surmounted by a cross flory, flanked by two cherub's heads, and with another in base
Qly, 1st and 4th, Swinburne, but tinctuers reversed, 2nd and 3rd, Spearman
Probably for Charlotte, dau. of Thomas Swinburne, who d.   (B.L.G. 5th ed.)

17. Dexter background black
Or a chevron rompu between three molets sable (Salt), impaling, Azure on a chevron or between three escallops argent a boar's head couped close sable between two estoiles gules (Moultrie)
Crest: On a chapeau azure and ermine a demi-ostrich wings expanded, in its beak a horseshoe or   Mantling: Gules and argent   Motto: Intemerata fides
Probably for Thomas Salt, who m. Harriett Moutrie at Shrewsbury, St Julian, 21 Aug. 1821.   (P.R.)

18. Dexter background black
Vert on a fess between three greyhounds' heads erased argent three crosses formy gules in chief a crescent argent (Muckleston), impaling, Ermine a lion rampant and a canton sable (Jefferies)
Crest: A greyhound's head erased proper collared gules   Mantling: Gules and argent   Motto: Fideliter   Cherub's head in base
For Edward Muckleston, of Shrewsbury, who m. Elizabeth Jefferies, of Willcot, and d. 21 June 1851.   (Burke's Commoners II, 169; M.I.)

19. All black background
Argent three boars' heads couped close sable langued gules (   )
No crest   Mantling: Gules and argent   Motto: In Deo solo confido
Half skull in top angle
Unidentified

20. Dexter background black
Qly per fess indented argent and sable (   ), impaling, Ermine three lozenges conjoined in fess sable (Pigott)
Crest: A talbot statant argent collared or   Mantling: Gules and argent
Motto: Mors janua vitæ
Unidentified

21. All black background
On an irregular lozenge flanked by two cherubs' heads and suspended by a lover's knot
Qly, 1st and 4th, Argent on a chevron azure three garbs or, on a canton gules a fret or (Eardley), 2nd and 3rd, Argent three lions rampant gules langued azure (   )
Unidentified

SHREWSBURY, Old St Chad's
1. All black background
Gules a chevron engrailed between three tigers' heads erased argent, the Badge of Ulster (Edwardes), impaling to the dexter, Or three chessrooks and chief embattled sable (Rocke), and to the sinister, Qly per fess

indented ermine and or ermined sable (Lacon)
Crest: A man's head in a helm affronté proper   Mantling: Gules and argent   On motto scroll: 1734
For Sir Francis Edwardes, 4th Bt., who m. 1st, Anne, dau. and co-heir of Thomas Rocke, and 2nd, Hester, dau. and co-heir of John Lacon, and d. (B.P. 1875 ed.)

2. All black background
Edwardes, impaling, Edwardes, in centre chief the Badge of Ulster
Crest and mantling: As 1.   Motto: In coelo quies
For Sir Henry Edwardes, 5th Bt., who m. Eleanor, dau. of Sir Francis Edwardes, 3rd Bt., and d. 1767.   (B.P. 1875 ed.)

3. All black background
On a lozenge   Argent a chevron between three stags' heads erased gules (Harwood), impaling, Vert on a fess between three greyhounds' heads erased argent three crosses formy gules (Muckleston)
Mantling: Gules and argent   Skull in base
For Anne, dau. of Edward Muckleston, of Pen-y-lan, who m. John Harwood, and d. 1702.   (B.L.G. 1853 ed.)

4. All black background
On a lozenge surmounted by a five-pointed crown
Sable a chevron between three battleaxes argent (Congreve), impaling, Argent a chevron between three stags' heads cabossed gules (Harwood)
Motto: Mors iter and vitam
For Abigail, dau. of John Harwood, who m. John Congreve, and d. 1752. (B.L.G. 1853 ed.)

5. All black background
Qly or and gules a bend sable (Clavering), impaling, Congreve
Crest: From a ducal coronet or a demi-lion rampant argent   Mantling: Gules and argent
Unidentified
(This hatchment was first recorded in 1954 and is now missing)

6. All black background
Ermine on a chief sable three escallops argent (Tayleur), impaling, Ermine on a fess sable a castle with two towers argent (Hill)
Crest: From a ducal coronet or a dexter arm in armour embowed in the hand a sword the point embrued proper   Mantling: Gules and argent
Motto: Firmitas in coelo   Skull in base
For William Tayleur, who m. Mary, sister of Sir Rowland Hill, of Hawkstone, and d. 6 May 1796.   (B.L.G. 5th ed.; M.I.)

Shropshire

7. All black background
Gules three demi-woodmen proper each holding a club over his dexter shoulder or (Wood of Shynwood)   To dexter of main shield, Wood, impaling, Per bend sinister ermine and sable a lion rampant or (   ) A.B1. To sinister of main shield, Wood   In pretence: Argent a chevron gules (   ) D.B1.
Crest: A swan wings expanded and inverted or   Mantling: Gules and argent   Motto: Serilis et otius
Unidentified

8. All black background
Gules a lion rampant argent between eight bezants (Heywick ?), impaling, Per chevron azure and or, in chief two eagles rising wings displayed and invected or (   )
Crest: A bull's head gules crowned or ?   Mantling: Gules and argent
A very small hatchment, c. 2 ft x 2 ft
Unidentified

9. Dexter background black
Ermine on a chief gules three lions rampant or (   )   To dexter of main shield, as above, impaling, Argent a molet sable a canton gules (Ashton) A.B1.   To sinister of main shield, as above, with in pretence: Argent on a bend gules three molets argent (   ) D.B1.
Crest: A tower or   Mantling: Gules and argent   Motto: In Deo solo confido   Skull in base
Unidentified

10. Dexter background black
Two oval shields   Dexter, within the Order of the Bath, Or a lion rampant reguardant sable langued and armed gules, on a chief embattled azure an Eastern view overprinted SEETABULDEE (Jenkins)   Sinister, within an ornamental wreath, as dexter, impaling, Argent on a chevron gules between three oak trees eradicated proper a boar's head couped close or (Spottiswoode)
Crest: From a mural coronet sable a lion passant reguardant crowned with an Eastern crown or, in the dexter paw a staff bearing a pennon gules inscribed NAGPORE   Mantling: Gules and argent   Motto: Perge sed caute   Supporters: Dexter, A Bengal Trooper, the exterior hand supporting a lance proper, the flag swallowtailed per fess gules and argent Sinister, A Madras Infantry Sepoy with musket and bayonet in position of support arms proper
For Sir Richard Jenkins, G.C.B., who m. 1824, Elizabeth Helen, dau. of Hugh Spottiswoode, and d. 20 Dec. 1853.   (B.L.G. 7th ed.)
(This hatchment was recorded in 1954 and is now missing)

11. All brown background
Or a raven sable (Corbet), impaling, Sable ten roundels four, three, two and one argent, on a chief argent a lion passant sable (Bridgeman)
Crest: An elephant argent tusked or caparisoned gules on his back a tower or   Mantling: Gules and argent   Motto: Deus pascit corvos
For Capt. Richard Corbet, who m. Judith, dau. of Sir John Bridgeman, Bt., and d. 1718.   (B.P. 1875 ed.)

12. All black background
Qly of twenty-three, 1st, Or a raven sable (Corbet), 2nd, Or an escarbuncle sable (Turet), 3rd, Azure two lions passant in pale or (Erdington), 4th, Gules a lion rampant or (Hopton), 5th, Azure a mermaid proper (Guros), 6th, Vairy argent and sable a canton gules (Stanton), 7th, Azure six lions rampant argent within a bordure engrailed or (Leybourne), 8th, Gules two lions passant in pale argent within a bordure engrailed or (Strange), 9th, Per bend azure and gules a bend between two crescents or (Loughbeigh), 10th, Barry of six sable and or, on a chief or two pallets sable, an escutcheon barry of six gules and ermine (Burley), 11th, Barry of six or and azure a bend gules (Pembruge), 12th, Or three roses gules barbed and seeded proper (Yonge), 13th, Or an eagle displayed vert debruised by a bend company argent and gules (Sibton), 14th, Barry nebuly of six argent and vert (Hawberke), 15th, Gules crusilly three lucies hauriant or (Lucy), 16th, Argent three chevronels sable (Archdeacon), 17th, Gules three roaches naiant in pale argent (Roche), 18th, Argent three bendlets sable (Haccombe), 19th, Gules a lion rampant within a bordure engrailed or debruised by a riband azure (Talbot), 20th, Barry of six or and vert each charged with three fleurs-de-lis counterchanged (Mortimer), 21st, Gules two bars vair (Saye), 22nd, Gules ten bezants, four, three, two and one (Zouch), 23rd, Argent an eagle displayed sable, over all a chevron gules charged with three roses argent (Humfreston)
Crest: An elephant argent armed or on its back a castle secured with straps or   Mantling: Gules and argent   Motto: Virtutis laus actio
In the dexter and sinister angles there are monograms of the initials S.V. and C.K.
A smaller than average hatchment, painted on wood
From the initials, probably for Sir Vincent Corbet, Kt., d. 8 Mar. 1622/3, and m. Frances, dau. and heiress of William Humfreston. His descendants with the christian name Vincent were Baronets and not Knights.
(Visit. Salop.)

13. All black background
Qly of twenty-two, 1st, Or a raven sable (Corbet), 2nd, Or an escarbuncle sable (Turet), 3rd, Azure two lions passant in pale or (Erdington), 4th, Gules crusilly a lion rampant or (Hopton), 5th, Azure a mermaid proper (Guros), 6th, Vairy argent and sable a canton gules (Stanton), 7th, Azure six lions rampant a bordure engrailed or (Leybourne), 8th, Gules two lions

passant in pale argent a bordure engrailed or (Strange), 9th, Per bend
azure and gules a bend between two crescents or (Loughbeigh), 10th,
Barry of six sable and or, on a chief or two pallets sable an escutcheon
ermine three bars gules (Burley), 11th, Barry of six or and azure a bend
gules (Pembruge), 12th, Or three roses gules barbed and seeded proper
(Yonge), 13th, Or an eagle displayed vert (Sibton), 14th, Barry nebuly of
six argent and vert (Hawberke), 15th, Gules crusilly three lucies hauriant
or (Lucy), 16th, Argent three chevronels sable (Archdeacon), 17th, Gules
three roaches naiant in pale argent (Roche), 18th, Argent three bendlets
sable (Haccombe), 19th, Gules a lion rampant debruised by a riband azure
within a bordure engrailed or (Talbot), 20th, Barry of six or and vert each
charged with three fleurs-de-lis counterchanged (Mortimer), 21st, Gules
two bars vair (Saye), 22nd, Gules ten bezants, four, three, two and one
(Zouch)
Crest: An elephant proper caparisoned gules on its back a castle or
Mantling: Gules and argent   Motto: Deus pascit corvos   Skull in
base
Unidentified

14. All black background

Qly of twenty-two, 1st, Or a raven sable (Corbet), 2nd, Or an escarbuncle
sable (Turet), 3rd, Azure two lions passant in pale or (Erdington), 4th,
Gules crusilly a lion rampant or (Hopton), 5th, Azure a mermaid proper
(Guros), 6th, Vairy argent and sable a canton gules (Stanton), 7th, Azure
six lions rampant or (Leybourne), 8th, Gules two lions passant in pale
within a bordure argent (Strange), 9th, Per bend azure and gules a bend
between two crescents or (Loughbeigh), 10th, Barry of six sable and or,
on a chief or two pallets sable an escutcheon barry of six ermine and
gules (Burley), 11th, Or two bars azure a bend gules (Pembruge), 12th,
Or three roses gules barbed and seeded proper (Yonge), 13th, Or an eagle
displayed vert, debruised by a bend compony argent and gules (Sibton),
14th, Barry nebuly of six or and vert (Hawberk), 15th, Gules crusilly
three lucies hauriant or (Lucy), 16th, Argent three chevronels sable
(Archdeacon), 17th, Gules three roaches naiant in pale argent (Roche),
18th, Argent three bendlets sable (Haccombe), 19th, Gules a lion rampant
debruised by a bend azure, all within a bordure engrailed or (Talbot),
20th, Or three bars sable (   ), 21st, Argent two bends wavy azure
(   ), 22nd, Gules ten bezants, four, three, two and one (Zouch)
Crest: An elephant proper on its back a tower secured with straps or
Mantling: Gules and argent   Motto: Deus pascit corvos   Skull on
each corner of the frame
Unidentified

15. Dexter background black

Qly, 1st, Or a raven sable, in chief the Badge of Ulster (Corbet), 2nd, Or
an escarbuncle sable (Turet), 3rd, Azure two lions passant in pale or

(Erdington), 4th, Gules crusilly a lion rampant or (Hopton), impaling, Sable a lion passant argent (Taylor)
Crests: Dexter, An elephant proper caparisoned gules on its back a tower or   Sinister, A squirrel sejant proper cracking a nut or   Mantling: Gules and argent   Motto: Deus pascit corvos
For Sir Andrew Corbet, 1st Bt., who m. 1790, Mary, eldest dau. of Thomas Taylor of Lymm Hall, Cheshire, and d. 6 June 1835.   (B.P. 1875 ed.)

16. Dexter background black
Qly of nine, 1st and 9th, Or a raven sable (Corbet), 2nd, Or an escarbuncle sable (Turet), 3rd, Azure two lions passant in pale or (Erdington), 4th, Gules crusilly a lion rampant or (Hopton), 5th, Gules two lions passant in pale argent a bordure engrailed or (Strange), 6th, Qly or and gules a bend sable (   ), 7th, Gules a lion rampant within a bordure engrailed or (Talbot), 8th, Vert billetty a lion rampant or (   ), impaling, Ermine on a fess sable a castle triple-towered argent (Hill)
Crests: Dexter, as 15., but with a motto on scroll above, Virtutis laus actio   Sinister, as 15., but with a motto on scroll above, Dum spiro spero   Mantling: Gules and argent   Motto: Deus pascit corvos
For Sir Andrew Vincent Corbet, 2nd Bt., who m. 1820, Rachel Stephens, eldest dau. of Col. John Hill, of Hardwicke, and d. Sept. 1855.   (B.P. 1875 ed.)
(This hatchment recorded in 1954 is now missing)

17. All black background
On an ornate curvilinear lozenge surmounted by a celestial crown
Or a raven sable (Corbet)
Motto: Virtus post funera vivit   Cherub's head on either side
Unidentified

18. All black background
On a decorative curvilinear lozenge
Qly, paly of six or and gules and ermine (Cotes), impaling, Or a raven sable (Corbet)
Motto: Virtus post funera vivit   Skull in base
For Elizabeth, dau. of Andrew Corbet, who m. the Rev. Washington Cotes, Dean of Lismore, and d. 1790.   (B.P. 1841 ed.)

19. All black background
Qly, 1st and 4th, Argent a lion rampant sable (Kynaston), 2nd, Gules a fess chequy argent and sable between six annulets or (Barker), 3rd, Or a raven sable (Corbet)
Crest: In front of the sun in splendour or an arm embowed in armour proper holding a sword argent hilted or   Mantling: Gules and argent
Motto: Deus est nobis sol et ensis
For Corbet Kynaston, who d. unm. 17 June 1740.   (B.L.G. 1853 ed.)

Shropshire

20. All black background
Argent a lion rampant sable armed and langued gules (Kynaston?)   In pretence: the same
No helm, crest, mantling or motto, but lavish gilt decoration surrounding shield, including a half-skull on each side in the angles of the hatchment
Possibly for William Kynaston, of Lee, who m. Jane Kynaston, and d. Aug. 1723, aged 92.   (M.I. at Ruyton XI Towns)

SHREWSBURY, St Julian

1. All black background
Paly of six argent and gules, on a bend sable three escallops or (Gibbons), impaling, Qly, 1st and 4th, Per chevron sable and ermine in chief two boars' heads couped close or (Sandford), 2nd and 3rd, Per fess gules and vert, a fess and in chief a chevron conjoined argent (Springseaux)
Crests: Dexter, An arm embowed in armour proper, garnished or, holding in the gauntlet a poleaxe or   Sinister, A boar's head couped close or with a broken spear azure headed argent thrust into his mouth
Mantling: Gules and argent tasselled or   A very small hatchment, c. 19 ins x 19 ins
For Richard Gibbons, Mayor of Shrewbury, who m. Anne, dau. of Humphrey Sandford, of Isle of Rossall, and d. 1650.   (Commoners II, 671)
(This hatchment is now missing)

2. All black background
Gules a chevron ermine between three mens' heads proper in helmets or, a martlet for difference (Morgan)
No crest, mantling or motto   Above the shield the date 1667, and on either side the letter R and M   A very small hatchment, c. 19 ins x 19 ins
Unidentified
(This hatchment is now missing)

3. All black background
Qly, 1st and 4th, Sable a chevron between three cocks argent combed and wattled or (   ), 2nd and 3rd, Gules a talbot salient argent (   )
Crest: A cock argent combed and wattled gules, membered or
Mantling: Gules and argent   Motto: Mors janua vitæ   Winged skull in base
Unidentified

4. All black background
Qly, 1st and 4th, Argent a cross flory engrailed sable between four choughs proper, on a chief azure a boar's head couped close argent (Owen), 2nd and 3rd, Argent a lion rampant sable (Owen)   In pretence: Or ermined sable a lion rampant and a canton sable (Jefferies)

Crest: Dexter, A chough proper, in the dexter claw a fleur-de-lis argent
Sinister, Two eagles' heads and necks conjoined or erased gules
Mantling: Gules and argent   Motto: God be my guide
For the Rev. Hugh Owen, who m. Harriet, dau. of Edward Jefferies, of Shrewsbury, and d. 23 Dec. 1827.   (B.L.G. 1853 ed.)

SHREWSBURY St George
1. All black background
Per chevron argent and gules a chevron counterchanged between in chief two garbs and in base a horse proper (Whitehurst), impaling, Argent a fess azure and in chief three martlets and in base a chevron azure (Tey)
Crest: An esquire's helm plumed argent with a lance passing through it
Mantling: Gules and argent   Motto: Je crains dieu
Unidentified

SHREWSBURY The Abbey Church
1. All black background
Qly, 1st and 4th, Azure a cinquefoil ermine (Astley), 2nd and 3rd, Ermine on a bend sable two hands and arms issuing out of clouds at the elbows proper rending a horseshoe or (Borlase), the Badge of Ulster   In pretence: Qly, 1st and 4th, Gules a saltire or surmounted by a cross ermine (Prince), 2nd and 3rd, Or a pale between four fleurs-de-lis gules (Gilly)
Crest: From a ducal coronet or a plume of three feathers argent
Mantling: Gules and argent   Motto: Fide sed cui vide
For Sir John Astley, 2nd Bt., M.P. for Shrewsbury, who m. Mary, dau. and heir of Francis Prynce and Mary, dau. and heir of Samuel Gilly, and d. 29 Dec. 1771.   (B.E.B.)

2. All black background
Or a lion's gamb in bend between two cross crosslets fitchy gules (Powys), impaling, Ermine on a fess sable three molets or (Lister)
Crest: A lion's gamb erased erect gules grasping a fleur-de-lis or
Mantling: Gules and argent   Motto: Memento mori
For Henry Powys, of the Abbey House, Shrewsbury, who m. 3rd, Dorothy, dau. of John Lister, of Sisonby, Leics., and d. 24 July 1774.   (B.L.G. 2nd ed.)

3. Sinister background black
Qly, 1st and 4th, Azure a fess between three falcons close argent (Philips), 2nd, Sable a lion rampant argent collared and chained or (Philips ?), 3rd, Gules two lions passant between nine cross crosslets fitchy or (Acton), impaling, Per pale or and sable a saltire engrailed counterchanged (Hunt ?)
Two cherubs' heads in top angle, and two others flanking shield; Winged skull in base
Unidentified

4. All black background
Arms: As 3.
Crests: Dexter, A demi-horse rampant argent   Sinister, A lion rampant argent collared and chained or   Mantling: Gules and argent
Motto: Ducit amor patria
Unidentified

STANTON-UPON-HINE-HEATH
1. Dexter background black
Or a raven proper in chief a crescent gules for cadency (Corbet), impaling, Argent on a bend sable between three choughs proper three garbs or (Wicksted)
Crest: An elephant argent and castle or   Mantling: Gules and argent
Motto: Deus pascit corvos
For Richard Prynce Corbet, of High Hatton, who m. Mary, dau. of John Wicksted, of Wem, and d. 30 Jan. 1779.   (B.P. 1875 ed.)

STIRCHLEY
1. All black background
Azure on a chevron between three unicorns' heads erased or three crescents gules (Clowes)
Crest: A demi-lion couped sable crowned or holding a battleaxe proper
Mantling: Gules and argent   Motto: Mors janua vitæ
Unidentified

WATERS UPTON
1. All black background
Qly of eight, 1st, Vert a chevron between three garbs or (Hatton), 2nd, Vairy argent and gules (   ), 3rd, Argent a cross flory between four martlets gules (Golborn), 4th, Argent an eagle displayed sable (Bruyn), 5th, Argent on a bend sable three covered cups argent (Rixton), 6th, Sable a cross engrailed ermine (Halom), 7th, Argent a saltire sable (for Hellesby), 8th, Sable a fess argent in chief a crescent for difference (Bostock)
Crest: On a mount vert a hind trippant proper   Motto: Virtus floret ubique
On a wood panel, c. 2 ft x 2 ft
Unidentified

WESTBURY
1. All black background
Argent on a chevron sable nine bezants (Severne)
Crest: A cinquefoil or   Mantling: Gules and argent   Motto: In coelo quies
For Lt.-Gen. John Severne, who d. unm. 6 July 1787, aged 89. (B.L.G. 2nd ed.; M.I.)

2. All black background
On a lozenge   Gules a lion rampant reguardant or (Pryce), impaling, Argent on a canton gules a gauntlet clenched proper (Topp)
For Jane, dau. of John Topp, who m.   Pryce, and d. 17 Nov. 1793. (B.L.G. 2nd ed.)

3. Dexter background black
Qly, 1st and 4th, Argent a bordure engrailed azure, on a canton gules a gauntlet clenched proper (Topp), 2nd and 3rd, Argent two bars gules, on a canton or a saltire sable (Broughton), impaling, Argent a chevron between three birds sable in the beak of each an ermine spot (Hughes)
Crest: A gauntlet holding a hand couped at the wrist dripping blood proper   Mantling and motto: As 1.
For Richard Topp, of Whitton, who m. 1790, Anne Hughes, of Shrewsbury, and d. 12 July 1829, aged 80.   (B.L.G. 2nd ed.)

4. All black background
Topp arms only, as 3.
No helm, crest or mantling, but shield surmounted by an urn
Probably for Edward Lingen Topp, who d. unm. at Whitton, 5 Dec. 1832, aged 37.   (B.L.G. 2nd ed.)

WILLEY

1. All black background
Qly, 1st and 4th, Qly per fess indented argent and gules in the first and fourth quarters a bugle-horn stringed sable (Forester), 2nd and 3rd, Azure a fess wavy ermine between three crescents argent (Weld)
Crest: A talbot passant argent eared gules gorged with a collar gules edged or charged with three bezants, lined or   Mantling: Gules and argent   Winged skull below
For George Forester, of Willey Park, who d. unm. 13 July 1811. (B.P. 1949 ed.)

2. Dexter background black
Qly, 1st and 4th, Qly per fess indented argent and sable in the first and fourth quarters a bugle-horn stringed sable (Forester), 2nd and 3rd, Azure a fess nebuly between three crescents ermine, in centre chief a cross crosslet fitchy or (Weld), impaling, Or two bars azure a chief qly azure and gules, the first and fourth quarters each charged with two fleurs-de-lis or, the second and third each with a lion passant guardant or (Manners)
Baron's coronet   Crests: Dexter, A talbot passant argent collared sable and chained or   Sinister, A wyvern sable goutty, winged, tufted, collared and chained or, and charged on the wing with an escallop sable
Mantle: Gules and ermine   Motto: Semper eadem   Supporters: Two talbots argent, collared and suspended from the collar a bugle-horn stringed sable, chained or

For Cecil, 1st Baron Forester, who m. 1800, Katharine Mary, 2nd dau. of Charles, 4th Duke of Rutland, and d. 23 May 1828.   (B.P. 1949 ed.)

3. Dexter background black
Qly, 1st and 4th, Qly per fess indented argent and sable in the first and fourth quarters a bugle-horn sable stringed and garnished or (Forester), 2nd and 3rd, Azure a fess embattled counter-embattled between three crescents ermine (Weld), impaling, Per pale, dexter, Azure two hare's heads couped or, sinister, Or a bunch of grapes between two vine leaves paleways proper (Maltzan)
Baron's coronet   Crests: Dexter, A talbot passant argent collared and chained sable   Sinister, A wyvern sable goutty, winged, collared and chained or   Motto: Semper eadem   Supporters: Two talbots argent, collared and chained sable, suspended from the collar a bugle-horn stringed and garnished or
For John George, 2nd Baron Forester, who m. 1856, Countess Alexandrina Julia Theresa Wilhelmina Sophia, dau. of Joachim Charles Louis Mortimer, Count von Maltzan, and d.s.p. 10 Oct. 1874.   (B.P. 1949 ed.)

WORFIELD

1. All black background
Argent a chevron between three cross crosslets fitchy sable (Davenport), impaling, Vert on a chevron argent three roses gules (Crawley)
Crest: A man's head couped at the shoulders in profile proper around the neck a rope or   Motto: Audaces fortuna juvet   On frame: V.Y.D. 20th Feb. 1834.
For William Yelverton Davenport, who m. Jane Elizabeth Crawley, of Bath, and d. 20 Feb. 1834.   (B.L.G. 1937 ed.; inscr. on hatchment)

2. Dexter background black
Davenport   In pretence: Argent three bendlets sable (Tongue)
Crest: As 1.   Motto: In coelo quies   Cherub's head below   On frame: E.S.D. 27th Feby 1842
For the Rev. Edmund Sharington Davenport, Vicar of Worfield, who m. 1807, Elizabeth, dau. of Joseph Tongue, of Hallon, and d. 27 Feb. 1842. (Sources, as 1.)

3. All black background
Qly, 1st and 4th, Davenport, 2nd and 3rd, Qly per fess indented gules and or (Bromley), impaling, Azure a sea-stag lodged argent (Marindin)
Crests: Dexter, as 1.   Sinister, A lion's gamb erased erect argent armed gules   Motto: As 1.   On frame: W.S.D. 1st Oct. 1871
For William Sharington Davenport, who m. 1835, Catherine Louisa, only dau. of Samuel Peter Marindin, of Chesterton, and d. 1 Oct. 1871. (Sources, as 1.)

WROCKWARDINE

1. All black background
Argent a chevron between three buckets sable hooped and handled or, a crescent for difference (Pemberton), impaling, Argent a chevron gules between three bears' heads erased sable (   )
Crest: A dragon's head couped sable dripping blood proper   Mantling: Gules and argent   Inscribed on base of hatchment: Edward Pemberton, ob. 19 July 1744: Mary Pemberton ob. 4 Jan. 1752.
(In view of inscription probably used for both husband and wife)

2. All black background
Pemberton, impaling, Qly 1st and 4th, Ermine a fret sable (Cludde), 2nd and 3rd, Argent a bend double cotised sable in chief a martlet sable (Orleton)
Crest: A dragon's head erased sable   Mantling: Gules and argent
Motto: In coelo quies   Winged skull in base   Inscribed on hatchment frame: Edward Pemberton, Esq. buried Dec. 5th, 1800, aged 75.
For Edward Pemberton, who m. Mary, dau. and heir of William Cludde, of Orleton, and d. 1800, aged 75.   (Inscr. on hatchment frame; B.L.G. 1871 ed.)

3. All black background
Qly, 1st and 4th, Cludde, 2nd and 3rd, Orleton
Crest: An eagle with wings expanded proper preying on a coney argent
Mantling: Gules and argent   Motto: In coelo quies
Inscribed on hatchment frame: Edward Cludde, d. 21st February 1785, aet 68.

WROXETER

1. Dexter background black
Qly, 1st and 4th, Ermine on a chief sable three escallops argent (Tayleur), 2nd and 3rd, Gules a lion rampant or within a bordure compony argent and sable (Skrymshire), impaling, Per bend sinister ermine and sable ermined argent a lion rampant or (Edwards)
Crest: Out of a coronet or an arm embowed in armour holding a sword in bend proper   Mantling: Gules and argent   Motto: Illegible
Unidentified

WALES
AND
MONMOUTHSHIRE

Llanbedrog 2: For Lt-Gen. Sir Love Parry Jones-Parry, 1853
(*Photograph courtesy of Mr. R. Barton*)

INTRODUCTION

This presentation of the section on the hatchments of Wales and Monmouth has been decided upon after some debate. There are 115 hatchments in Wales not counting a further 20 in the old county of Monmouth. It seemed impractical to present a section on each of the old Welsh counties (or even the new counties) because the numbers were so few. Equally some people had argued that Monmouth was an English county and not a Welsh one and so should be listed separately. The result is a compromise in that all Welsh hatchments are grouped together in alphabetical order of location but with those of Monmouth grouped together as a sub-section within 'Wales'. (To enable the student to find the hatchments a list of locations by old and new counties is included as an appendix.)

This decision has the added advantage of keeping the hatchments of the Morgan family of Tredegar grouped together. Of the 19 Monmouth hatchments, 17 are for the Morgan family and connections. At Lower Machen there are the hatchments for Thomas Morgan d. 1769, his wife, three sons, one daughter-in-law and four of the grand-children, or their spouses, of his daughter Jane. Jane's own hatchment is at Bassaleg with those of four of her children and/or spouses and her grandson Charles, 1st Baron Tredegar.

The only 'old' county which has more hatchments than Monmouth is Denbigh. There are 12 in Denbigh parish church to various families and six at St George to the family and predecessors of the 1st Baron Dinorben. There are three more for the Baron's family on Anglesea at Llanwenllwyfo. The other location with a high number of hatchments is Welshpool Museum (Powysland) which has fourteen. These came to the Museum from a number of locations. It holds one for the 3rd Earl Powis d. 1891 for which there are further hatchments at Cardiff Folk Museum and Llandidloes. Three hatchments surviving for one individual is unusual. One further point of note is the 63 quarterings at Llanbedrog (see photograph opposite).

In many cases the identification of hatchments and especially quarterings was not straightforward. In Welsh heraldry many different families use the same arms. Heraldry was not used widely in Wales until the Tudor times. At this date arms were assigned to a number of Welsh Royal and Noble Families (or 'Tribes'). This resulted in people with different 'surnames' using the same arms. Just one example is the arms 'Per bend sinister ermine and sable ermined argent a lion rampant or' which represent Mostyn at Llanelltyd and Llandudno and Trevor at Llansantffraid-Glyn-Ceiriog.

The recording of these hatchments has been the result of the effort of several correspondents. This may have introduced, to the eyes of people knowledgeable about Welsh Heraldry, some inconsistencies. The same arms used as a quartering may be identified with a 'surname' in one place and with a tribal name elsewhere.

Thanks are due to the many correspondents who have recorded these hatchments over a period of 40 years. I also appreciate the efforts of Miss Preen, Anthony Jones, Richard Jones, Dr. Derek Llewellyn, and David Phillips who have checked the majority between them.

JOHN E. TITTERTON
7 Cecil Aldin Drive, Tilehurst, Reading

MONMOUTHSHIRE

ABERGAVENNY

1. Dexter background black
Argent a chevron gules between three bulls' heads couped sable (Bullen), impaling, Per fess argent and gules a fess wavy between three crescents counterchanged (Springett)
Crest: A bull's head couped proper   Mantling: Gules and argent   Motto: Resurgam
Unidentified

BASSALEG

1. Sinister background black
Two shields   Dexter, Qly, 1st and 4th, Or a griffin segreant sable (Morgan), 2nd and 3rd, Or on a chevron azure between three roses sable three thistles slipped or (Gould) the Badge of Ulster   Sinister, as dexter, with Morgan in pretence
Motto: Vivit post funera virtus
Two cherubs' heads above and palm branches and skull below
For Jane, dau. of Thomas Morgan, of Tredegar, who m. Sir Charles Gould, 1st Bt., and d. 14 Feb. 1797.   (B.P. 1939 ed.)

2. Sinister background black
Qly, as 1., with Badge of Ulster   In pretence: Or on a bend sinister azure three escallops or (Stoney)
Motto: Virtus vincit
For Mary, only child of George Stoney, who m. 1791, Sir Charles Morgan, 2nd Bt., and d. 24 Mar. 1808.   (B.P. 1939 ed.)

3. All black background
Arms: As 2.
Crest: From a ducal coronet or a reindeer's head couped or attired gules
Mantling: Gules and argent   Motto: Si Deus nobiscum quis contra nos
For Sir Charles Morgan, 2nd Bt., who d. 5 Dec. 1846.   (B.P. 1939 ed.)

4. All black background
Arms: as 2.
Crest: As 3.   Mantling: Argent and gules   No motto
Also for Sir Charles Morgan, 2nd Bt., who d. 5 Dec. 1846.   (B.P. 1939 ed.)

5. All brown background
Qly, 1st and 4th, Or a griffin segreant sable (Morgan), 2nd and 3rd, Or on a chevron azure between three roses sable three thistles or (Gould), impaling, Per pale gules and sable on a cross argent five lozenges vert (Mundy) Baron's coronet   Crest: A reindeer's head couped argent attired gules Motto: Si Deus nobiscum quis contra nos   Supporters: Dexter, A lion sable charged on the shoulder with a thistle slipped or   Sinister, A griffin sable charged as dexter   All on a mantle
For Charles, 1st Baron Tredegar, who m. 1827, Rosamund, only dau. of General Godfred Basil Mundy, and d. 16 Apr. 1875.   (B.P. 1939 ed.)

6. All black background
Gules a cross flory ermine (Homfray), impaling two coats per pale, 1st, Azure on a cross or quarter pierced azure four round buckles gules (Ball), 2nd, Or on a chevron azure between three roses gules three thistles slipped or (Gould)
For Jane (who was previously married to Capt. Henry Ball, R.N., who d. 1792), dau. of Sir Charles Morgan, 1st Bt., who m. Samuel Homfray, of Penydarron, and d. 22 Dec. 1846.   (B.P. 1875 ed.)

ITTON

1. All black background
Qly of six, 1st, Argent on a fess between three cross crosslets sable three martlets or (Curre), 2nd, Chequey or and gules a fess ermine (Turberville), 3rd, Gules three chevrons argent (Morgan Garn), 4th, Sable a cross floretty between twelve billets argent (Norris), 5th, Argent a unicorn within a bordure engrailed sable (Lewis), 6th, Or a lion rampant sable (Mathew)
Crest: An eagle displayed or   Mantling: Gules and argent   Motto: Gratus si amicus
Possibly for William Curre, who d. 20 Feb. 1855. His wife Mary Bushby had died in 1823.   (B.L.G. 1871 ed.)

LOWER MACHEN

1. Sinister background black
Qly, 1st, Or a griffin segreant sable (Morgan), 2nd, Gules a lion rampant or (Meredith ap Bleddyn), 3rd, Argent three bulls' heads cabossed sable (Bleddri ap Cadifor Fawr), 4th, Sable a boar argent his head gules collared and chained or browsing under a holly bush (Llowarch Llawen Vaur)   In pretence: Qly, 1st and 4th, Or chevron between three estoiles gules (Colchester), 2nd and 3rd, Argent on a bend engrailed azure a cross crosslet fitchy or (Clarke)
Crest: A reindeer's head couped or attired gules   No helm or mantling Motto: Mors janua vita
Inscribed on frame: Jane, wife of Thomas Morgan, Esq., M.P. died 1767, aged 64
For Jane, dau. and co-heir of Maynard Colchester, of Westbury-on-Severn, who m. Thomas Morgan, of Tredegar, and d. 5 Nov. 1767.   (B.P. 1939 ed.)

Wales and Monmouthshire 75

2. All black background
Arms: As 1.
Crest: A reindeer's head or   Mantling: Gules and argent   Motto: In coelo quies
Inscribed on frame: Col. Thomas Morgan, Esqr. M.P. of Tredegar died 1769, aged 67
For Thomas Morgan, who m. Jane, dau. of Maynard Colchester, and d. 12 Apr. 1769.   (B.P. 1939 ed.)

3. All black background
Qly of six, 1st and 6th, Morgan, 2nd, Meredith ap Bleddyn, 3rd, Bleddri ap Cadifor Fawr, 4th, Llowarch Llawen Vaur, 5th, Colchester
Crest: A buck's head proper   Mantling: Gules and argent   Motto: In coelo quies   Skull and crossbones in base
Inscribed on frame: Col. Thomas Morgan, M.P. of Tredegar died 1774, aged 44
For Col. Thomas Morgan, of Tredegar, who d. unm., 15 May 1771.   (B.P. 1939 ed.)

4. Sinister background black
Qly of six. As 3.   In pretence: Argent a fess between three lozenges sable (Parry)
No helm or crest   Motto: In coelo quies
Inscribed on frame: Mary, wife of Charles Morgan, died 1777 aged 42
For Mary, dau. and heir of Thomas Parry, who m. Charles Morgan, of Tredegar, and d.s.p. 24 June 1779.   (B.P. 1939 ed.)

5. All black background
Qly of nine, 1st and 9th, Morgan, 2nd, Meredith ap Bleddyn, 3rd, Bleddri ap Cadifor Fawr, 4th, Llowarch Llawen Vaur, 5th, Azure a chevron between three lion's heads erased or (Wyndham), 6th, Sable a fess argent between three boy's heads couped at the shoulder, around the neck of each a snake vert (Vaughan), 7th, Colchester, 8th, Clarke   In pretence: Parry
Crest: On a wreath or and sable a reindeer's head or   Peer's mantle
Motto: In coelo quies
Inscribed on frame: Charles Morgan Esqr. M.P. of Tredegar, died 1787, aged 51
For Charles Morgan, who m. Mary, dau. and heir of Thomas Parry, and d.s.p. 24 May 1787.   (B.P. 1939 ed.)
(There is another hatchment for Charles Morgan at St Weonards, Herefordshire)

6. Dexter background black
Qly of nine, as 5., impaling, Argent on a chevron gules between three hunting-horns sable stringed gules three cross crosslets fitchy or (Burt)
Crest: A reindeer's head proper   Mantling: Gules and argent   Motto: Deus nobiscum quis contra nos

Inscribed on frame: John Morgan, Esq. M.P. of Tredegar, died 1792, aged 52
For John Morgan, of Tredegar, who m. Louisa, dau. of Charles Pym Burt, and d.s.p. 1792. (B.P. 1939 ed.)

7. All black background
Qly, 1st and 4th, Morgan, 2nd and the 3rd, Or on a chevron between three roses sable three thistles or (Gould), impaling, Sable a cross patonce within a bordure or (Lascelles)
Crest: A reindeer's head or attired gules   Mantling: Gules and argent
Inscribed on frame: Revd. Augustus Morgan, died 1875.
For the Rev. Charles Augustus Samuel Morgan, Rector of Machen, who m. Frances, dau. of Rowley Lascelles, and d. 5 Sept. 1875.   (B.P. 1939 ed.)

8. Sinister background black
Arms: As 7.
No helm, mantling or motto
Inscription on frame: Francis, wife of Revd. A. Morgan, died 1867.
For Frances, wife of the Rev. Charles Augustus Samuel Morgan, d. 16 Feb. 1867.   (B.P. 1939 ed.)

9. All black background
Azure a snake nowed or between three sinister gauntlets argent (Milman), impaling, Qly, 1st and 4th, Or a griffin segreant sable (Morgan), 2nd and 3rd, Or on a chevron between three roses sable three thistles or (Gould)
Crest: A stag couchant per pale argent and or attired or ermined sable charged with two roundels azure   Motto: Si Deus nobiscum quis contra nos   Flags and cannon on either side of shield and medal pendent below displaying campaign bars for the Pensinsular War.
Inscription on frame: Lieut. General Milman, died 1856, aged 73. For Lt.-Gen. Francis Milman, who m. 1817, Maria Margaretta, dau. of Sir Charles Morgan, 2nd Bt., and d. 9 Nov. 1856.   (B.P. 1939 ed.)

10. All black background
On a lozenge   Sable a cross patonce a bordure or (Lascelles)
Inscribed on frame: Anna Lascelles, died 1862.
Possibly for Anna, sister of No 8.   (B.P. 1939 ed.)

11. Identical to No. 6

WONASTOW

1. Dexter background black
Qly, 1st and 4th, Argent a cross moline square pierced sable (   ), 2nd and 3rd, Ermine on two bars gules six pierced mullets or (Bavant)   In pretence: Qly, 1st and 4th, Sable a chevron between three garbs or (   ), 2nd and 3rd, Argent a chevron gules between three bulls' heads

couped sable (Bullen)
Crest: A demi-lion rampant proper holding between the paws a cross moline as in the arms   Mantling: Gules and argent   Motto: Val gallo
Unidentified

WALES
BETTWS (see page 107)
CAPEL LLANILTERNE

1. Dexter background black
Qly, 1st and 4th, Sable three garbs or (Price), 2nd and 3rd, Gules three chevronels or (for Williams)   In pretence: Argent on a chevron gules between three bugle-horns sable stringed gules as many cross crosslets fitchy or (Birt)
Crest: A Paschal Lamb proper   Mantling: Gules and argent   Motto: In coelo quies
For John Price, of Park and Llandough Castle, who m. Jane, dau. and co-heir of Peter Birt, of Wenvoe Castle, and d. 16 June 1818, aged 67. (M.I.)

2. All black background
On a lozenge
Arms: As 1.
For Jane, widow of John Price, d. 5 Dec. 1819.   (M.I.)

CARDIFF Welsh Folk Museum, St Fagans

1. All black background
Per pale azure and gules three lions rampant argent (Herbert)
Earl's coronet   Crest: A wyvern vert holding in the mouth a sinister hand couped gules   Motto: Ung je serviray   Supporters: Dexter, An elephant argent   Sinister, A griffin argent wings expanded charged with five molets in saltire azure
For Edward James, 3rd Earl of Powis, b. 5 Nov. 1818, d. unm. 7 May 1891.   (B.P. 1939 ed.)
(There are similar hatchments at Llanidloes and Welshpool Museum.)

2. All black background
Qly, 1st and 4th, Argent a cross flory engrailed sable between four Cornish choughs (Edwards, from Edwin of Tegaingle), 2nd, Gules a lion rampant holding between the paws a rose argent (   ), 3rd, Sable on a chevron or between three martlets argent three bugle-horns sable (   )
Crest: Out of a ducal coronet or a demi-lion rampant argent   Mantling: Or, gules and argent   Motto: In coelo quies
Unidentified
(Donated to the museum by Miss Joan Griffiths of Dinas Powis, South Glamorgan, 1935)

3. Sinister background black
Qly, 1st and 7th, Gules on a bend argent a lion passant sable (Davies, from Cynric Effel), 2nd, Gules a lion rampant reguardant or ( ), 3rd, Or four pales gules (Lloyd of Yale), 4th, Sable three pierced mullets argent (Spurstow?), 5th, Sable three roses argent barbed and seeded proper (Cunedda Wledig), 6th, Argent a chevron engrailed between three heronshaws sable (Henshaw), 8th, Sable a lion rampant argent (... from Cydrich nap Gwaethfoed), In pretence: Qly, 1st and 4th, Quarterly gules and or four lions passant guardant counterchanged, ( ), 2nd and 3rd, Azure a fess ermine between three lions rampant or ( )
Motto: Gloria deo The shield is surmounted by a winged cherubs head above a celestial crown
Unidentified
(Donated by Major T. H. Davies-Colley of Newbold, Chester, 1931)

CHIRK

1. Dexter background black
Qly, 1st and 4th, Argent on a bend vert three wolves' heads erased argent (Myddelton), 2nd and 3rd, Vert an eagle displayed and a canton argent (Biddulph), impaling, Qly, 1st, qly i & iv, Per pale sable and argent on a chaplet four quatrefoils all counterchanged (Nairne), ii, Or on a fess gules between in chief three crosses patty gules and in base a mullet azure three bezants (Mercer), iii, Argent a chevron sable between three boars' head erased gules armed argent langued azure (Elphinstone), 2nd, qly i & iv, Ermine on a bend azure a magnetic needle pointing at the pole star or (Petty), ii & iii, Argent a saltire gules and a chief ermine (Fitzmaurice), 3rd, qly i & iv, Paly of six or and sable (Atholl), ii, Or a fess chequy azure and argent (Stewart), iii, Azure three mullets argent within a double tressure flory counter-flory or (Murray), 4th, Argent three martlets sable on a comble azure a cross or a franc quartier azure charged with a sword palewise argent hilted and pommelled or (Flahault), in centre a crescent gules.
Crests: Dexter, A dexter hand couped proper Sinister, A wolf salient argent charged on the shoulder with a trefoil slipped gules
Mantling: Vert and argent Motto: In veritate triumpho
For Lt. Col. Ririd Myddelton, L.V.O., J.P., D.L., of Chirk Castle, who m. Lady Mary Margaret Elizabeth, sister of the 8th Marquess of Lansdowne, and d. 7 Feb. 1988.
This hatchment was painted by Mr Peter Spurrier, then Portcullis Pursuivant and hung in the church in early 1993.

CLYRO

1. Dexter background black
Argent a chevron gules between three roundels azure (Baskerville), impaling, Gules seven lozenges conjoined vair, three, three, one (Guise)
Crest: A wolf's head erased or pierced through the mouth with an arrow

in bend sinister point upwards gules   Mantling: Gules and argent
Motto: Spero ut fidelis
For Thomas Baskerville Mynors-Baskerville, of Clyro Court, who m. 2nd, 1837, Elizabeth Mary, dau. of the Rev. Powell Guise, and d. 9 Sept. 1864.   (B.L.G. 1937 ed.)
(The current whereabouts of this hatchment is unknown)

DENBIGH, Old Church

1. All black background

On a lozenge surmounted by two cherubs' heads
Qly, 1st and 4th, Argent on a bend vert three wolves' heads erased argent (Myddelton), 2nd and 3rd, Azure a bridge with three arches proper (Turbridge ?) In pretence: Argent a chevron between three lozenges sable ermined argent (Shaw)
Mantling: Gules and argent   Motto: In coelo quies
For Catherine, dau. of Thomas Shaw, who m. William Myddelton, of Gwaynynog, and d. 12 Aug. 1776. (Pedigree of Myddelton of Gwaynynog, Myddelton 1910)
(In very poor condition when recorded in 1957 and is now missing)

2. All black background

On a lozenge suspended from a bow
Qly, 1st and 4th, Myddelton, with a bend azure, 2nd, Azure a bridge or on a weir surmounted by a pennon argent (Turbridge ?), 3rd, Shaw
Motto: In coelo quies   Two cherubs' heads above,   Winged skull in base and massive golden urn as background to lozenge
For Maria Sydney Myddelton, dau. of William and Catherine Myddelton, who d. June 1793.   (Source, as 1.)

3. Dexter background black

Qly, 1st and 4th, Myddelton, 2nd, Azure a bridge on a weir proper, on the bridge a flagpole with pennon gules (Turbridge ?), 3rd, Shaw, impaling, Argent six bees volant three, two and one proper (Wynne)
Crest: From a ducal coronet or a dexter hand proper   Motto: In coelo quies   On a mantle gules and ermine,   Winged skull in base
For Rev. Robert Myddelton, who m. Catherine, dau. of Robert Wynne, of Plas Heaton, and d. 27 Dec. 1808.   (Source, as 1.)

4. Dexter background black

Myddelton, impaling, Argent a lion passant guardant gules regally crowned or (Ogilvie)
Crest and motto: As 3.   Mantling: Gules and argent
For Robert Myddelton, of Gwaynynog, D.D., Rector of Rotherhithe, who m. 1794, May, only surviving child of Capt. James Ogilvie, and d. 7 Dec. 1815.   (B.L.G. 1853 ed.)

5. Dexter background black

Qly, 1st and 4th, Myddelton, 2nd, Azure a bridge on a weir proper in chief a label argent (Turbridge ?), 3rd, Shaw, impaling, Azure a chevron between three covered cups or (Butler)
Crest: A dexter hand proper   Mantling and motto: As 4.   Skull in base
For Col. John Myddelton, who m. Mary, dau. of William Butler, of Flintshire, and d. 29 Dec. 1792.   (Source, as 1.)

6. Dexter background black

Argent on a bend engrailed sable three stags' heads cabossed argent attired or (Heaton), impaling, Azure two bars and in chief three pierced molets argent (Venables)
Crest: A stag's head cabossed argent attired or   Mantling: Gules and argent
Motto: Non omnis moriar
For Richard Heaton, of Plas Heaton, who m. 1783, Sarah, dau. of Edward Venables, of Oswestry, and d. 27 Nov. 1791.   (B.L.G. 1937 ed.)
(In very poor condition when recorded in 1959 and is now missing)

7. All black background

On an asymmetrical lozenge surmounted by an escallop
Heaton, impaling, Azure two bars and in chief three molets argent (Venables)
Mantling: Gules and argent   Motto: In coelo quies   Skull in base
For Sarah, widow of Richard Heaton, who d. 21 Apr. 1814.   (B.L.G. 1937 ed.)

8. Sinister background black

Qly, 1st and 4th, Heaton, 2nd, Argent three cross crosslets fitchy sable (Adamson), 3rd, Or a lion rampant sable a bordure engrailed gules (   ), impaling, Qly, 1st and 4th, Argent three boars' heads couped sable langued gules (for Jones), 2nd and 3rd, Sable a wolf rampant and in chief three estoiles argent (Wilson)
Mantling: Gules and argent   Motto: In coelo quies   Skull in base
For Elizabeth, dau. of John Jones, of Cefn-Coch, who m. 1814, as his 1st wife, John Heaton, of Plas Heaton, and d. 15 Aug. 1822.   (B.L.G. 1937 ed.)

9. Dexter background black

Gules a lion rampant ducally crowned between three crescents or (Salusbury), impaling, Sable three battleaxes, heads argent (   )
Crest: Two lions respectant ducally crowned holding between them a crescent or   Mantling: Gules and argent   Mottoes: Sat est prostrasse leoni; and below this: In coelo quies   Skull in base
Unidentified

10. All black background

On a lozenge surmounted by a skull   Arms: As 9.
Mantling: Gules and argent   Motto: In coelo quies   Crossbones below
Unidentified

11. All black background
Azure a greyhound's head couped argent between three mascles or (Clough), impaling, Argent a chevron between three boars' heads couped sable langued gules (Lloyd)
Crest: A demi-lion in the dexter paw a sword argent   Mantling: Gules and argent   Motto: In te Domine speravi   Skull in base
For the Rev. Thomas Clough, Rector of Denbigh, who m. Dorothea, dau. of Howel Lloyd, of Wygfair and Hafodunos, and d. 1814.   (B.L.G. 2nd ed.)
(In very poor condition when recorded in 1957 and is now missing)

12. All black background
Qly, 1st, Sable a hart trippant argent attired and unguled or (Lloyd), 2nd, Azure floretty or a lion rampant gules (   ), 3rd, Ermine a lion rampant sable (   ), 4th, Sable on an escutcheon argent a cross gules between four doves sable (   )
Crest: A stag trippant proper attired or   Mantling: Gules and argent
Motto: Resurgam   Two cherubs' heads above and skull below
Unidentified

ERDDIG

1. Dexter background black
Argent on a saltire azure a bezant (Yorke), impaling, Azure semy-de-lis a lion rampant reguardant argent (Holland)
Crest: A lion's head erased proper collared gules, on the collar a bezant
Mantling: Gules and argent   Motto: In cruce salus
For Simon Yorke, of Erddig, who m. Margaret, dau. of John Holland, of Teyrdan, and d. 12 Dec. 1834.   (B.L.G. 1871 ed.)

GRESFORD

1. All black background
Qly, 1st and 4th, Ermine a rose gules barbed and seeded proper (Boscawen), 2nd and 3rd, Per bend sinister ermine and sable ermined argent a lion rampant or (Trevor), impaling, Qly, 1st and 4th, Argent on a bend sable three chessrooks argent (Bunbury), 2nd and 3rd, Argent a fess between three pewits gules (Stanney)
Crest: A boar passant gules armed or   Mantling: Gules and argent
Motto: Spes mea in Deo
For George Boscawen, who m. Annabella, 2nd dau. of the Rev. Sir William Bunbury, Bt., and d. 14 Oct. 1833.   (B.P. 1939 ed.)

2. Dexter background black
Argent a lion passant sable armed and langued gules between three fleurs-de-lis gules (Griffith), impaling, Argent on a chevron gules three annulets or (Bond)   In pretence (over line of impalement): Qly, 1st and 4th, Boscawen, 2nd and 3rd, Trevor

Crest: A lion passant sable armed and langued gules   Mantling: Gules and argent   Motto: Mors janua vitæ

For Thomas Griffith, of Trevalyn Hall, who m. 1st, 1813, Catherine (d. 14 Jan. 1814), dau. of William Bond, and 2nd, 1830, Elizabeth Mary, dau. of William Boscawen, and d. 9 July 1856.   (B.L.G. 5th ed.; M.I.)

HAVERFORDWEST St Mary's

1. Dexter background black

Argent a lion rampant sable ducally gorged and chained or, the Badge of Ulster (Philips), impaling, to the dexter, Qly, 1st, Azure three boars' heads couped or (Gordon), 2nd, Or three lions' heads erased gules (Badenoch), 3rd, Or three crescents within a doubled tressure gules (Seton), 4th, Azure three cinquefoils argent with a bordure embattled argent flory counter-flory (Fraser), and to the sinister, Qly, 1st and 4th, Gules a bend between six cross crosslets fitchy argent on a canton azure a sun in splendour or (Howard), 2nd and 3rd, Argent a chevron gules between three bulls' heads sable (Boleyne)

Baron's coronet   Crest: A lion as in the arms   Motto: Ducit amor patriæ   Supporters: Two horses argent each charged on the breast with five ermine spots in saltire.

For Richard, 1st Baron Milford, who m. 1st, Eliza, only dau. of John Gordon, of Hanwell. She d. 24 Mar. 1852. He m. 2nd, Lady Anne Howard, dau. of the 4th Earl of Wicklow, and d.s.p. 3 Jan. 1857. (B.P. 1855 ed.; B.E.P. 1883 ed.)

2. Sinister background black

Philipps, impaling, Qly, 1st, Gordon, 2nd, Badenoch, 3rd, Seton, 4th, Fraser

Baron's coronet   No crest or motto   Supporters: As 1.

For Eliza, 1st wife, of Richard, 1st Baron Milford. She d. 24 Mar. 1852. (B.P. 1855 ed.)

KERRY

1. Dexter background black

Per pale azure and gules three lions rampant argent (Herbert)   In pretence: Qly, 1st and 4th, Argent a cross engrailed floretty between three choughs sable, on a chief azure a boar's head argent (Owen), 2nd and 3rd, Argent a lion rampant and a canton sable (Owen)

Crest: A wyvern vert ducally gorged with chain reflexed or   Mantling: Gules and argent   Motto: Fortitudine et prudentia

Winged skull in base

For John Herbert, of Dolforgan, who m. 1772, Avarina Brunetta, dau. and heiress of Thomas Owen, of Llunllo, Mont., and d. May 1807. (B.L.G. 1937 ed.)

2. Dexter background black

Qly, 1st and 4th, Herbert, 2nd and 3rd, Owen qly as 1., impaling, Argent

a saltire sable, on a chief gules three cushions argent (Johnson)
Crest, mantling and motto: As 1.
For John Owen Herbert, of Dolforgan, who m. 1823, Harriet, dau. of the Rev. Charles Johnson, of South Stoke, Somerset, and d. 31 Mar. 1824, aged 41.   (B.L.G. 1937 ed.)

3. Sinister background black
Sable a lion rampant between eight cross crosslets argent (Long)   In pretence: Qly, 1st and 4th, Herbert, 2nd and 3rd, qly i. & iv. Argent a cross moline between four choughs sable, on a chief azure a boar's head argent (Owen), ii. & iii. Argent a lion rampant sable a canton gules (Owen)
Three cherubs' heads above shield
For Harriet Avarina Brunetta, dau. of John Owen Herbert, of Dolforgan, who m. Walter Long, of Rood Ashton, and d. 26 Jan. 1847.   (B.L.G. 1937 ed.)
(This hatchment was in poor condition when recorded in 1953, and is now missing)

LLANAFAN

1. Dexter and top half sinister background black
Qly, 1st and 4th, Sable a chevron between three fleur-de-lis argent (the ensigns of Collwyn ap Tangno, Lord of Efionydd, (Vaughan)), 2nd and 3rd, Argent on a fess gules three eagles heads' erased sable three escallop shells or (Wilmot), impaling, two coats per fess, in chief, Sable an eagle displayed argent beaked and legged or within a bordure engrailed argent (Palk), in base, Sable a fess between three mascles or (Mitchell)
Earl's Coronet   Crest: An armed arm embowed proper holding a fleurs-de-lis argent   Mantling: Gules and argent   Motto: Non revertar inultus   Supporters: Dexter, A dragon reguardant wings endorsed vert, gorged with a collar sable edged argent charged with three fleurs-de-lis argent with a chain or   Sinister, A unicorn reguardant argent maned tufted and unguled or with collar and chain as dexter
For Ernest August, 4th Earl of Lisburne, who m. 1st, Mary, dau. of Sir Lawrence Palk, Bt., and 2nd, Elizabeth, dau. of Col. Hugh Henry Mitchell and d. 8 Nov. 1873   (G.E.C.)

2. Dexter and top half sinister background black
Vaughan, impaling two coats per fess, in chief, Argent two bars and in chief a lion passant guardant gules (Burnaby), in base, Ermine on a fess gules a lion passant or (Probyn)
Earl's Coronet   Crest, Motto and Supporters: As 1
For Ernest Augustus Malet, 5th Earl of Lisburne, who m. 1st, Laura Gertrude, dau. of Edwyn Burnaby, of Baggrave Hall, Leics., and 2nd, Alice Dalton, dau. of Edmund Probyn, and d. 31 Mar. 1888   (G.E.C.)

LLANBEDROG

1. All black background
Qly of six, 1st, Ermine a lion rampant sable (Jones), 2nd, Azure three crowns in pale or (Beli Mawr), 3rd, Sable three horses' heads argent (Lloyd), 4th, Per bend sinister ermine and sable ermined argent a lion rampant or (Trevor), 5th, Gules a lion rampant or a bordure argent (   ), 6th, two coats per fess, in chief, Argent a chevron sable on a chief sable three martlets argent (Wylde), in base, Gules a lion rampant or (   )   In pretence: Qly of six, 1st, Argent a fess between three lozenges sable (Parry), 2nd, Azure a stag trippant argent (Parry), 3rd, Azure a chevron between three fleurs-de-lis or (   ), 4th, Gules a savage's head affronté couped proper (Marchudd), 5th, Or a raven sable (Corbet), 6th, Sable a chevron between three lions rampant or (   )
Crests: Dexter, A demi-lion gules   Sinister, A horse's head argent
Mantling: Gules and argent   Motto: Mors janua vitæ   Cherubs above and winged skull in base
For Thomas Parry Jones-Parry, son of John Jones, who m. 1781, Margaret, dau. and co-heir of Love Parry. He assumed the additional name of Parry and d. 1835.   (B.L.G. 1937 ed.)

2. Dexter and top half sinister background black
Qly of sixty-three, 1st and 63rd, Ermine a lion rampant sable (Jones of Lynon), 2nd, Sable a chevron between three fishes hauriant argent (Jones of Gartherne), 3rd, Azure three crowns in pale or (Beli Mawr), 4th, Sable three nags' heads argent (Lloyd), 5th, Per bend sinister ermine and sable ermined argent a lion rampant or (Tudor Trevor), 6th, Gules a lion rampant or a bordure argent (Everard), 7th, Gules a lion rampant or, on a chief argent a chevron beneath a fess sable (Hughes of Cefn Llanfair), 8th, Argent a fess between three lozenges sable (Parry), 9th, Vert a stag trippant proper (Parry of Modryn), 10th, Sable a chevron between three fleurs-de-lis argent (Bodwa, Prince of Powis), 11th, Gules a Saracen's head erased proper wreathed round the temples proper (Marchudd), 12th, Qly gules and or four lions passant counterchanged (Mervyn, Prince of Powis), 13th, Gules and lion rampant a bordure indented or (Howell Dda), 14th, Sable a chevron between three dolphins naiant argent (Williams of Dendraeth), 15th, Argent a chevron azure between three nags' heads erased sable (Jones of Castle March), 16th, as 10th, 17th, Gules a chevron ermine between three Saracens' heads couped proper (Williams), 18th, Or a lion rampant reguardant sable (Gwaeth Voed), 19th, Gules a chevron between three lions rampant or (Awfa of Cynddelw), 20th, Gules a chevron between three roses argent slipped proper (Enion ap Geraint), 21st, Argent a chevron between three crows sable in the beak of each an ermine spot (Llowarch ap Bran), 22nd, Gules a chevron argent between three stags' heads cabossed argent (Griffith), 23rd, Or a raven proper (Corbet), 24th, Argent an escarbuncle sable (Turrett), 25th, Azure two lions passant or (Erdington), 26th, Gules a lion rampant within an orle of nine cross crosslets fitchy or (Hopton), 27th,

Gules a mermaid in her hand a mirror proper (Guros), 28th, Vair a canton gules (Stanton), 29th, Azure six lions rampant argent a bordure engrailed or (Leybourne), 30th, Gules two lions passant argent a bordure engrailed or (Strange), 31st, Per bend gules and azure over all a bend between two crescents or (Loughbeigh), 32nd, Sable three bars or on a chief or two pallets sable, on an inescutcheon ermine three bars gules twelve cinquefoils or (Burley), 33rd, Barry of six or and azure a bend gules (Penbruge), 34th, Or three roses gules barbed proper (Young), 35th, Or an eagle displayed vert debruised by a bend compony argent and gules (Sibton), 36th, Barry nebuly or and vert (Hawberke), 37th, Barry of six or and vert each bar charged with three fleurs-de-lis counterchanged (Mortimer), 38th, Gules two bars vair (Saye), 39th, Gules ten bezants four, three, two and one or a label azure (Zouche), 40th, Gules crusily or three lucies hauriant argent (Lucy), 41st, Argent three chevronels sable (Archdeacon), 42nd, Gules three roaches naiant fesswise in pale or (Roach), 43rd, Argent three bends sable (Haccombe), 44th, Gules a lion rampant or within a bordure indented or debruised by a bend azure (Talbot), 45th Argent an eagle displayed vert, over all a chevron gules charged with three roses or (Humfreston), 46th and 18th, 47th, Sable a lion rampant argent (Griffith of Cydryth), 48th, Sable three fleurs-de-lis or (Wynn), 49th, Or a griffin segreant vert (Effin of Gwyddno), 50th, Gules a griffin segreant or (Lewis of Gwyufe), 51st, Ermine on a saltire gules a crescent or (Wynne of Peniarth), 52nd, Ermine on a saltire gules a molet or (Yale), 53rd, as 19th, 54th, as 22nd, 55th, as 21st, 56th, Argent on a bend sable three leopards' faces argent (Gwierydd ap Rhys Goch), 57th, as 10th (   ), 58th, as 18th, 59th, Gules on a chevron ermine between three helms argent a crescent or (Owen of Meredith), 60th (   ), as 10th with crescent for difference, 61st, Qly i. & iv. Argent a double-headed eagle displayed sable, ii. & iii. Argent three ragged staffs gules fired proper, on an inescutcheon argent a man's leg couped a la quise sable (Cilmsn Troed-Du), 62nd as 56th, impaling two coats per fess, 1st, Or on a bend vert three leopards' faces or (Stevenson of Binfield), 2nd, Qly i. & iv. Vert a stag's head erased or a crescent for difference, ii. & iii. Per pale or and azure on a chief gules three leopards' faces or (Caldecott)

Knights' helm   Crests: 1. Three battleaxes proper   2. A demi-lion rampant gules   3. A stag trippant argent attired or   4. A horse's head erased argent   5. A naked cubit arm proper holding a fleur-de-lis vert
Mantling: Gules and argent   Badge of Order of Hanover   Mottoes: above crests: Heb dduw heb ddim duwadigon   below shield: Gofal dyn duw ai gwerid

For Lt.-Gen. Sir Love Parry Jones-Parry, K.H., of Madryn, who m. 1st, 1806, Sophia, only dau. of Robert Stevenson, of Binfield, Berks., and 2nd, 1826, Elizabeth, only dau. of Thomas Caldecott, of Holton, Lincs., and d. 25 Jan. 1853.   (B.L.G. 1937; M.I.)

N.B. This hatchment has been restored since the photograph on page 70 was taken.

LLANBETHIAN

1. All black background
Qly, 1st and 4th, Argent a chevron gules between three lions rampant sable (Bourne), 2nd, Barry of six azure and or and in chief three mascles or (Spurling), 3rd, Azure two bars and in chief three mascles or (Spurling)
Crest: A lion passant argent   Mantling: Gules and argent   Motto: Nosce te ipsum
Unidentified

LLANDUDNO, Gloddaeth Hall School

1. All black background
Qly, 1st, Per bend sinister ermine and sable ermined argent a lion rampant or (Tudor Trevor), 2nd, Argent a cross engrailed floretty sable between four choughs proper (   ), 3rd, Gules a chevron between three roundels argent (Madoc Gloddeth), 4th, Argent six lions rampant sable (Savage), over all the Badge of Ulster, impaling, Qly, 1st and 4th, Argent a chevron between three griffins passant sable (Finch), 2nd and 3rd, Gules three lions rampant or (Fitzherbert)
No helm, crest or mantling   Motto: Auxilium meum a domino
For Sir Roger Mostyn, 3rd Bt., who m. 1703, Essex, dau. of Daniel, Earl of Winchelsea and Nottingham, and d. 5 May 1739.   (B.P. 1939 ed.)

2. All black background
Qly of six, 1st four quarters, as 1., 5th Vert fretty or (Whitmore), 6th, Argent a bend between two wolves' heads erased sable (   ), on the 1st quarter the Badge of Ulster
Crest: A lion rampant or   Mantling: Gules and argent   Motto: As 1.
Probably for Sir Thomas Mostyn, 4th Bt., who m. 1735, Sarah, dau. and co-heir of Robert Western, and d. 24 Mar. 1758

3. All black background
Qly of nine, 1st four quarters, as 1., 5th, Vert three eagles displayed or (Wynne), 6th, Or on a saltire gules a crescent argent (Vaughan ?), 7th, Gules a chevron or a chief ermine (   ), 8th, Sable chevron or between three fleurs-de-lis argent (Vaughan), 9th, Argent three palets vert a bordure engrailed or (   )
Crest: A lion rampant or   Mantling: Gules and argent   Motto: Resurgam
For Sir Thomas Mostyn, 6th Bt., M.P. for Flints, d. unm. 17 Apr. 1831. (B.P. 1949 ed.)

4. Dexter background black
Qly, 1st, qly i. & iv. Per pale argent and sable a lion rampant gules a bordure engrailed sable, the Badge of Ulster (Champneys), ii. & iii. Per bend sinister ermine and sable ermined argent a lion rampant or a canton

azure (Mostyn), 2nd, Chequy argent and gules on a bend sable three lions passant or (Chandler ?), 3rd, Gules three bells or (Swymmer), 4th, Per pale argent and or a wyvern sable breasts and wings gules (Wilkins ?)   In pretence: Qly of eight, 1st, Per bend sinister ermine and sable ermined argent a lion rampant or (Mostyn), 2nd, Argent a cross floretty sable between four choughs proper (   ), 3rd, Gules a chevron between three roundels argent (Madoc Cloddeth), 4th, Argent six lions rampant sable (Savage), 5th, Vert fretty or (Whitmore), 6th, Barry or and azure a bend gules (Gaunt ?), 7th, Argent a bend between six bees sable (Beeston), 8th, Mostyn
Three crests   1. A demi-man proper holding   2. Out of a coronet or a sword gules point upwards between two wings dexter gules, sinister azure   3. A lion rampant gules   Peer's mantling   Motto: Pro patria non timidus perire   Supporters: Two lions gules collared or pendant therefrom an escutcheon, dexter with the arms of Navarre, sinister with arms of France
For Sir Thomas Swymmers Mostyn Champneys, 2nd Bt., who m. 1792, Charlotte, dau. of Sir Roger Mostyn, 5th Bt., and d.   (B.P. 1939 ed.)

5. All black background
On a lozenge Qly, 1st and 4th, Champneys, 2nd and 3rd, Mostyn, in the 1st quarter the Badge of Ulster   In pretence: Qly of eight, as 4.
Motto: Mors janua vitæ
For Charlotte, widow of Sir Thomas Champneys, d. 1845.   (B.P. 1939 ed.)

LLANDYBIE

1. Dexter background black
Per fess sable and argent a lion rampant counterchanged (Vaughan ?), impaling, Per pale azure and gules three lions rampant argent (Herbert)
Crest: A lion rampant sable   Mantling: Gules and argent   No motto
For Sir Henry Vaughan of Derwith, who m. Elizabeth, dau. of William Herbert, of Coldbrooke, and d. 36 Dec. 1676, aged 63.   (M.I.)

LLANDYFRIOG

1. Dexter background black
Qly, 1st, Argent a cross engrailed sable (Fitzwilliams), 2nd, Barry of eight gules and or ermined sable over all three escutcheons argent (Hall of Cilgwyn), 3rd, Gules on a chevron argent between three talbots' heads collared erased or three bluebells proper (Hall), 4th, Gules on a chevron argent three cross crosslets fitchy sable (Brathwaite)
Crest: A demi-lion rampant or holding a sword wavy erect proper
Mantling: Gules and argent   Mottoes: (above crest) Vive ut vivas, (in base) Coelum quid querimus ultra
Inscribed on frame: Charles Home Lloyd Fitzwilliams, of Cilggwyn, 1843-1925.

For Charles Home Lloyd Fitzwilliams who m. Margaret Alice, dau. of
David Russell Crawford, of Cheltenham, and d. 14 May 1925.   (M.I.)
(A very small hatchment, c. 2 ft x 2 ft)

LLANDYRNOG
1. Dexter background black
Qly, 1st and 4th, Argent a harvest fly between three roses gules in centre chief an ancient crown or (Pounderling), 2nd and 3rd, Gules a lion rampant or (Williams of Vron Iw), impaling, Qly, 1st and 4th, Azure three crossbows argent (Robarts), 2nd and 3rd, Azure a chevron ermine between three Cornish choughs proper (   )
No helm   Crest: A demi-lion rampant or holding a rose or slipped proper   Mantling: Gules and argent   Motto: In coelo quies
Skull and crossbones in base
c. 3 ft x 3 ft, very worn, now framed and glazed
For John Madocks, of Vron and Glanywern, who m. Sidney, dau. of Abraham Roberts, and d. 1837. She d. 1852.   (per J. Tindale)

LLANELLTYD
1. All black background
Qly, 1st, Qly i. & iv. Or ermined sable a lion rampant gules, ii. & iii. Gules a lion rampant or (Vaughan), 2nd, Or a lion rampant azure (Nanney), 3rd, Vert a goat passant argent (   ), 4th, Gules a chevron ermine between three Saxons' heads couped in profile proper (Williams), over all the Badge of Ulster, impaling, Per bend sinister ermine and sable ermined argent a lion rampant or (Mostyn)
Knight's Helm   Crest: A lion rampant azure armed and langued gules gorged with an antique coronet or   Mantle: Gules and argent
Motto: In coelo quies   Cherub's head above and skull below
For Sir Robert Williams Vaughan, 2nd. Bt., who m. 1801, Anna Maria, sister and co-heir of Sir Thomas Mostyn, Bt., and d. 22 Feb. 1843.
(B.L.G. 1849 ed.)

LLANFAIR-AR-Y-BRUN
1. All black background
Qly of six, 1st, Sable a fess or between two swords in pale points outwards argent pommelled and hilted or (Gwynne), 2nd, Or three bats wings displayed proper (   ), 3rd, Sable a chevron between three spearheads argent (Games), 4th, Argent a chevron sable between three choughs proper a bordure gules bezanty (Johnes), 5th, Gules a lion rampant reguardant or langued azure (Gwynne), 6th, Argent three boars' heads couped sable langued gules (   ), impaling, Argent a chevron azure between three oak leaves vert fructed or (Smythies)
Crest: A dexter gauntleted hand sable holding a dagger proper hilted or imbrued gules piercing a boar's head or langued gules   Mantling: Gules and argent   Motto: Vim vi repellere licet
For Sackville Henry Frederick Gwynne, of Glanbrane, who m. 1st, 1796,

Mary Anne, dau. of Francis Smythies, and 2nd, Sarah Antoinette Simes, of Kensington, and d. 8th Sept. 1836. (B.L.G. 1937 ed.)

2. Sinister background black
Arms: As 1.
Motto: Resurgam   Cherub's head above and skull below
For Mary Anne, dau. of Francis Smythies, 1st wife of Sackville Henry Frederick Gwynne, d. 1816. (B.L.G. 1937 ed.)

LLANFOR

1. All black background
Qly, 1st and 4th, Gules a lion rampant argent (Price), 2nd and 3rd, Argent a Tudor rose proper (   ), impaling, Per bend sinister ermine and sable ermined argent a lion rampant or (Lloyd)
Crest: A lion rampant argent holding a rose gules   Mantle: Gules and argent   Motto: Vita brevis gloria aeterna
Probably for Richard Watkin Price, of Rhiwlas, who m. 1801, Frances, dau. of John Lloyd, and d. 14 June 1860. (B.L.G. 1937 ed.)

LLANGEDWYN

1. Dexter background black
Two circles, on the breast of an eagle displayed or   Dexter, Qly of six, 1st, Vert three eagles displayed in fess or (Wynn), 2nd, Argent two foxes counter salient in saltire gules (Williams), 3rd, Per fess sable and argent a lion rampant counterchanged (Kyffin), 4th, Gules a chevron argent between three boars' heads or (Thelwall), 5th, Azure a cross paty fitchy argent (Cadwallader), 6th, Gules three lions passant in pale or (Gruffyd ap Cynan) The Badge of Ulster in chief of 2nd quarter   Sinister, Qly, 1st and 4th, Vert three eagles displayed in fess or (Wynn), 2nd and 3rd, Argent two foxes counter salient gules (Williams)
No helm, crest or mantling   Motto: Eryr eryrod eryri
For Sir Watkin Williams-Wynn, 6th Bt., who m. 1852, Mary Emily, youngest dau. of the Rt. Hon. Sir Henry Watkin Williams-Wynn, and d. 9 May 1885. (B.P. 1939 ed.)
(There is a duplicate hatchment at Welshpool Museum)

LLANGIAN

1. Dexter background black
Qly, 1st and 4th, Paly of eight argent and sable (Edwards), 2nd and 3rd, Gules a chevron argent a chief ermine (   )   In pretence: Qly of six, 1st, Gules a lion rampant a bordure engrailed or (Lloyd), 2nd, Azure a chevron ermine between three dolphins embowed argent (   ), 3rd, Sable three eagles displayed in fess or (   ), 4th, Azure a chevron argent between three fleurs-de-lis or (   ), 5th, Azure a chevron ermine between three horses' heads erased argent (   ), 6th, Gules three human heads in profile couped at the shoulders proper (   )

Crest: An arm embowed in armour holding a fleur-de-lis azure
Mantling: Gules and argent   Motto: Duw a diwedd dda
For Richard Edwards, who m. Annabella, only dau. and heiress of Richard Lloyd, of Bronhauloc and d. 26 July 1830.   (M.I.)

2. All black background
On a lozenge surmountd by a cherub's head
Arms: As 1.   Motto: Resurgam
For Annabella, widow or Richard Edwards. She d. 15 Nov. 1831, aged 62. (M.I.)

LLANGOEDMOR

1. All black (greenish blue) background
Qly, 1st and 4th, Sable a spearhead erect argent embrued gules between three scaling ladders bendwise argent (Lloyd), 2nd and 3rd, Qly, i. & iv. Argent a lion rampant gules (   ), ii. & iii. Azure a lion rampant between eight cinquefoils or (   )
Crest: A lion rampant or   No helm or mantling   Motto: Fide et fortitudine   On wood   Shield attached to hatchment
Probably either for Thomas Lloyd, d. 21 Sept. 1810, or his son Thomas, d. 12 July 1859. (M.I.)

LLANGOLLEN

1. All black background
On a lozenge   Argent a lion rampant sable (Price)
Motto: In Colo quies   Cherub's head at each side of lozenge and skull in base
For Susanna, dau. of the Rev. David Price, of Glynn, who d. 5 Oct. 1795, aged 31.   (M.I.)

LLANGOLLEN, Trevor Chapel

1. Dexter background black
Qly, 1st, qly i. & iv. Gules a lion rampant reguardant or (Thomas), ii. & iii. Argent three boars' heads sable (Thomas), 2nd, Argent on a cross sable five crescents or in dexter chief a spear's head sable (Gwilliam), 3rd, Argent a chevron between three ravens sable each holding an ermine spot in its beak (Lloyd), 4th, Gules a chevron or a chief ermine (Lloyd)
In pretence: Qly, 1st, Argent a cross flory engrailed sable between four Cornish choughs (Lloyd), 2nd, Azure a lion rampant argent langued gules (   ), 3rd, Sable three horses' heads argent (Lloyd), 4th, Per bend sinister ermine and sable ermined argent a lion rampant or (Trevor)
Crest: A stag's head erased proper attired or   Mantling: Or and gules
Motto: Oriens morior moriens orior
For Rice Thomas, of Trevor Hall, who m. Margaret, dau. of John Lloyd, and d. 17 Nov. 1814, aged 68.   (M.I.)

2. All black background
On a lozenge surmounted by cherubs' heads
Qly, 1st and 4th, Gules a lion rampant reguardant or (Thomas), 2nd and 3rd, Argent three boars' heads sable (Thomas)   In pretence: Qly, 1st and 4th, Argent a cross flory engrailed sable between four Cornish choughs (Lloyd), 2nd and 3rd, Trevor
Skull below
For Margaret, widow of Rice Thomas, who d. 20 April 1826.   (M.I.)

LLANIDLOES
1. All black background
Per pale azure and gules three lions rampant argent (Herbert)
Earl's coronet   Crest: A wyvern vert   No mantling   Motto: Ung je serviray   Supporters: Dexter, An elephant argent   Sinister, A griffin wings expanded argent ducally gorged gules and charged with five molets sable
Probably for Edward James, 3rd Earl of Powis, who. d. unm. 7 May 1891.   (B.P. 1963 ed.)
(There are similar hatchments at Welshpool Museum and at Cardiff Welsh Folk Museum)

LLANNANNO
1. All black background
Qly, 1st and 4th, Argent three boars' heads sable (for Stephens), 2nd and 3rd, Gules a lion rampant reguardant or (Stephens ?)
Crest: A dexter arm proper, the hand holding a sword argent hilted or on which is transfixed a griffin's head sable   Mantling: Gules and argent
Motto: Semper liber   c. 2 ft x 2 ft
For John Stephens, of Castle Vale, High Sheriff of Radnorshire, who d. 1875. (note affixed to hatchment)

LLANNON
1. Dexter background black
Gules a chevron ermine between three men's heads couped at the shoulders in profile and in armour proper (Griffiths)
Crest: An oak tree proper   No mantling   Motto: Resurgam
c. 2 ft 6 ins x 2 ft 6 ins   Skull and crossbones in base
For Charles Griffith Griffiths, of Marcholgllyn, who m. Eliza, dau. of Robert Walters, and d. 11 June 1850.   (M.I.)

LLANRHAIDR-YM-MOCHNANT
1. Sinister background black
On a lozenge surmounted by three cherubs' heads
Qly, 1st and 4th, Argent a chevron vert between three palmers' staves and

scrips sable garnished gules (Palmer), 2nd and 3rd, Chequy argent and azure on a chief gules three annulets or (   ), in chief the Badge of Ulster   In pretence: Sable a lion rampant or (Matthews)
Supporters: Two panthers reguardant proper, breathing smoke, collared and chained or, pendant from each collar an escutcheon, Or a Passion cross gules between two palm branches in saltire vert
For Elenora, dau. and co-heiress of John Matthews, of Eyarth and Plas Bostock, co. Denbigh, who m. Sir William Henry Roger Palmer, 4th Bt., of Castle Lackin, co. Mayo, and d. 1852.   (B.P. 1855 ed.)

2. Dexter background black
Qly, 1st and 4th, Gules a chevron between three molets or (Roberts), 2nd and 3rd, Or a lion rampant gules (Roberts)   In pretence: Azure three lions rampant or, on a chief argent three cross crosslets sable (Matthews)   Crest: indecipherable   Mantle: Gules and argent   Motto: Deus pascit corvos
For the Rev. Nathaniel Roberts, of Cefn Park, co. Denbigh, who m. Frances, sister of Elenora and co-heiress of John Matthews, and d.
(B.P. 1855 ed.)

3. All black background
On a lozenge surmounted by three cherubs' heads
Qly, as 2.   In pretence: Azure three lions rampant or, on a chief sable three cross crosslets or (Matthews)
Motto: Mors janua vitæ   Winged skull in base
For Frances, widow of the Rev. Nathaniel Roberts, who d.   (B.P. 1855 ed.)

LLANSANTFFRIAD-GLYN-CEIRIOG
1. Sinister background black
Qly, 1st and 4th, Per bend sinister ermine and sable ermined argent a lion rampant or (Trevor), 2nd and 3rd, Gules on a fess sable between three lions passant or three escallops argent (Hill), impaling, Qly, 1st and 4th, France and England quarterly, 2nd, Scotland, 3rd, Ireland, over all a baton sinister compony argent and azure (Fitzroy)
Viscount's coronet   No helm, crest, mantling or motto
For Charlotte, dau. of Charles, 1st Lord Southampton, who m. 1795, Arthur, 2nd Viscount Dungannon, and d. 22 Nov. 1828.   (B.P. 1855 ed.)

LLANSTEPHAN
1. All black background
Argent a ship with three masts proper sails furled sable, in dexter chief a fleur-de-lis sable (Meares), impaling, Azure a chevron or ermined sable between three griffins' heads erased sable beaked argent (Gardner)
Crest: A mermaid with comb and glass proper   Mantling: Argent (very slight)   Motto: Omnia fortunas committo
On a wood panel c. 3 ft x 3 ft
For George Mears, who m. Hannah Gardner, and d. 6 Apr. 1833, or Hannah his wife, who d. 13 Apr. 1833.   (M.I.)

2. Identical to 1.
As George and his wife died only seven days apart, this hatchment is probably for the other party.

LLANTWIT MAJOR
1. Dexter background black
Gules a pelican on her nest, wings displayed and vulning herself proper (Carne)
Crest: A pelican displayed with two heads issuing from a ducal coronet proper
Mantling: Gules and argent   Motto: (over crest) En toute loyale
(below shield) Fy-ngobaith-sydd-yn-nuw
Inscribed around shield as follows. Dexter chief: Granted A.D. 1336
Sinister chief: Confirmed A.D. 1842   To dexter: The Rev. Robert Carne, M.A. of Nash Manor and Dimland House   To sinister: who died ye 10th of November 1849, aged 86 years and 7 months
An exceptionally large hatchment
For the Rev. Robert Carne (formerly Nicholl), who m. 2nd, 1800, Elizabeth, dau. and heir of Capt. Charles Carne. He took the name and arms of Carne on his marriage, and d. 10 Nov. 1849.   (B.L.G. 2nd ed.)

LLANWENLLWYFO
1. Dexter background black
Qly, 1st and 4th, Gules two lions passant between three roses argent (Hughes), 2nd, Azure a chevron between three lions rampant or (for Lewis), 3rd, Or on a bend sable three men's heads proper (   ), impaling, two coats per fess, in chief, Barry of six argent and azure on a bend gules three bezants (Grey), and in base, Argent on a bend between two unicorns' heads erased azure three mascles or (Smyth)
Baron's coronet   Crest: From a crown vallary or a demi-lion argent holding a pike proper   Motto: Rhad Duw a Rhyddid   Supporters: Dexter, An ancient Briton in his dexter hand a pike proper   Sinister, A dragon vert (pink wings), charged on the shoulder with a rose argent   All on a mantle gules and ermine
Black felt on wide frame
For William, 1st Baron Dinorben, who m. 1st, Charlotte, dau. of Ralph William Grey. She d. 21 Jan. 1835. He m. 2nd, 1840, Gertrude, youngest dau. of Grice Smyth, of co. Waterford, and d. 10 Feb. 1852.   (B.L.G. 1937 ed.)
(There is another hatchment for Baron Dinorben at St George)

2. All black background
On a lozenge   Dexter, Qly as 1. with field of 2nd quarter sable, impaling, Smyth
Baron's coronet   Supporters: As 1.
For Gertrude, widow of William, 1st Baron Dinorben. She d. 3 Jan. 1871.
(Source, as 1.)

3. Dexter background black
Argent on a cross azure four fleurs-de-lis or, the Badge of Ulster (Neave)
In pretence: Gules two lions passant between three roses argent (Hughes)
Crest: From a ducal coronet or a lily proper   Mantling: Vert and argent   Motto: Sola proba quae honesta
For Sir Arundell Neave, 4th Bt., of Dagnam Park, Essex, who m. 1871, Gwen Gertrude, only child of William, 1st Lord Dinorben, and d. 21 Sept. 1877.   (B.L.G. 1937 ed.)

LLANYNYS

1. Dexter background black
Gules a chevron or between three men's heads in profile proper (Edwards), impaling two coats per fess, In chief, Qly, 1st and 4th, Sable a chevron between three boars' heads argent (Price), 2nd and 3rd, Argent a cross floretty between four birds sable (   ) In base, Gules on a bend argent a lion passant sable (for Lloyd)   In pretence: Qly, 1st, Argent two foxes counter salient in saltire gules (Williams), 2nd, Per fess argent and sable a lion rampant counterchanged (Kyffin), 3rd, Gules a chevron between three lions rampant argent (Owen), 4th, Gules three demi-lions rampant or (Bennet)
No helm   Crest: From a ducal coronet or a demi-fox gules
Mantling: Gules and argent   Motto: In coelo quies   Winged skull in base
For the Rev. William Williams, who m. Jennet, dau. of Edward Edwards. Edward Edwards m. Lowry, dau. of Griffith Price, by his wife, Jonnett, heiress, of David Lloyd of Braichy Clunant. The Rev. William Williams took the name and arms of Edwards, and d. 27 Jan. 1828.   (M.I.)

2. All black background
Arms: As 1., with demi-lions for lions in Owen quarter
Mantling: Gules and argent   Motto: In coelo quies   Skull and crossbones in base
Shield (only) has been repainted
For Jennet, widow of the Rev. William Williams Edwards, who d. 8 Aug. 1859, aged 84.   (Source as 1.)

MACHYNLLETH

1. Dexter background black
Two cartouches   Dexter, within the ribbon of the Order of St Patrick, Qly, 1st and 4th, Azure three sinister gauntlets or (Vane), 2nd and 3rd, Or a bend countercompony argent and azure between two lions rampant gules (Stewart)   Sinister, within an ornamental wreath, as dexter, impaling, Qly, 1st and 4th, Qly gules and or a fess between four lions passant guardant all counterchanged (Edwards), 2nd and 3rd, Sable on a fess between in chief a lion rampant argent and in base a fleur-de-lis or, two snakes interlaced proper (Owen)

Marquess's coronet   Three crests: 1. A dragon statant or (Stewart)
2. A dexter cubit arm in armour the hand grasping a sword proper hilted or (Vane)   3. A griffin's head erased per pale argent and sable (Tempest)   Badge of the Order of St Patrick pendent below cartouches   Motto: Nec temere nec timide   Supporters: Two hussars of the 10th regiment, the dexter mounted on a grey horse, the sinister upon a bay horse, with their swords drawn, and accoutred all proper
For George, 5th Marquess of Londonderry, K.P., who m. 3 Aug. 1846, Mary Cornelis, only dau. and heiress of Sir John Edwards, Bt., of Garth, and d. 6 Nov. 1884.   (B.P. 1939 ed.)

MARGAM Abbey
1. Dexter background black
Gules a lion rampant within a bordure engrailed or (Talbot), impaling, Qly, 1st and 4th, Sable two lions passant in pale paly of six argent and gules (Strangways), 2nd, Ermine on a chevron azure three foxes' heads erased or, on canton azure a fleur-de-lis or (Fox), 3rd, Sable three talbots passant argent (Horner)
Crest: On a chapeau a lion statant tail extended or   Mantling: Gules and or
For Thomas Mansel Talbot of Margam, who m. 1794, Mary Lucy, 2nd dau. of Henry, 2nd Earl of Ilchester, and d. 1813.   (B.L.G. 2nd ed.; M.I.)

2. Sinister background black
Talbot, impaling, Qly, 1st and 4th, qly, i. & iv. Argent a cross upon three steps gules and on the cross the figure of Christ crucifed or (Butler of Cahir), ii. Per fess indented sable and or (for Butler), iii. Gules three covered cups or a crescent for difference (Fitzgerald), all within a bordure ermine (Butler, Earl of Glengall), 2nd, Per pale indented or and gules (Periers), 3rd, Argent a double-headed eagle displayed sable between three crosses formy gules (   )
For Lady Charlotte, dau. of Richard, 1st Earl of Glengall, who m. Christopher Rice Mansel Talbot, and d. 1846.   (M.I.)

MONTGOMERY
1. All black background
Per pale azure and gules three lions rampant argent (Herbert)
Earl's coronet   Crest: A wyvern vert with a hand gules in its mouth   Mantle: Gules and ermine   Motto: Fortitudine et prudentia
Supporters: Dexter, A lion argent collared or, pendent there from an escutcheon 'Or a lion's gamb erased in bend gules'   Sinister, A panther guardant argent collared or semy of roundels azure, or and gules, pendent from the collar an escutcheon, 'Or a lion rampant gules'
For George Herbert, 2nd and last Earl of Powis, who d. unm. 16 Jan. 1801. (B.P. 1939 ed.)

MYDDFAI

1. All black background
Qly, 1st and 4th, Argent on a mount vert a greyhound passant sable collared or (Holford), 2nd and 3rd, Sable a fess cotised or between two swords argent hilted or the one in chief point upwards the one in base downwards (Gwynne)   In pretence: Qly of twelve, 1st Gwynne, 2nd, Or three heads cabossed sable (   ), 3rd, Sable a chevron between three spearheads argent (Davy Gam), 4th, Sable a lion rampant holding a ... argent (   ), 5th, Sable a chevron between three ... argent (   ), 6th, Argent three boars' heads sable (Blayney), 7th, Gules a lion rampant reguardant or (Gwynne of Garth), 8th, Argent a chevron gules between three birds sable a bordure engrailed gules (Johnes ?), 9th, Sable a chevron between three fleurs-de-lis or (Hughes), 10th, Argent a wyvern's head erased holding a hand gules (   ), 11th, Argent a bend sinister between ... sable (   ), 12th, Sable a stag passant argent between the antlers ... gules (   )

Crests: Dexter, Arising from a sun gules a greyhound's head sable   Sinister, A cubit arm in armour issuant from a crescent or the hand holding a sword erect argent hilted or impaling a boar's head or   Mantling: Gules and argent   Motto: Toujours fidele   Winged skull below

For Col. James Price Holford, who m. Anna Maria, dau. and heir of Roderick Gwynne, of Buckland, and d. Aug. 1846.   (B.L.G. 1937 ed.)

Nanteos House, Nr. Aberystwyth

1. All black background
Qly, 1st, Argent a cross florrety engrailed sable between four Cornish choughs proper on a canton sable a chevron or between three spear heads argent (Powell), 2nd, Sable a lion passant or between three fleur-de-lis argent (North ?), 3rd, Per fess or and sable (   ), 4th, Argent three boars' heads couped close sable (Owen ?)

Crest: A talbot's head erased argent collared or   Mantling: Gules and argent   Motto: Inter hastas et hostes

Unidentified

(There may be further hatchments at Nanteos' which is no longer open to the public)

NEATH

1. All black background
Gules a fess between three water bougets ermine (Miers)
Crest: A plume of ostrich feathers   Mantling: Gules and argent
Motto: Requiescat in pace   Skull below
Unidentified

2. Dexter background black
Miers, impaling, Ermine on a fess cotised in base sable a triple-towered castle argent (Hill)
Crest and mantling as 1.   Motto: Resurgam
For John Nathaniel Miers, of Cadoxton Lodge, who m. Mary, dau. of Richard Hill, of Court y Ralla, and d. 19 Aug. 1814, aged 40.   (M.I.; Neath Antiquarian Society Trans. 1937-1939)

3. All black background
On a lozenge   Arms as 2 with field of impaled arms argent   Skull below
For Mary, widow of 2., who d. 25 July 1824.   (Sources, as 2.)

4. All black background
On a lozenge
Miers, with bougets argent, impaling, Argent on a bend sable in chief an oakleaf proper (Cock)
Probably for Rachel, widow of Nathaniel Miers (d. 1782). She d. 8 June 1827, aged 86.   (M.I.)

5. All black background
Qly, 1st and 4th, Per pale indented sable and ermine on a chevron gules five crosses paty or (Mackworth), 2nd and 3rd, Gules three chevronels argent (Evans), in chief the Badge of Ulster, impaling, Miers as 4.
Crest: Indecipherable   Mantling: Gules and argent   Motto: Resurgam
For Sir Robert Humphrey Mackworth, 2nd Bt., who m. Mary-Anne, dau. of Nathaniel Miers, of Neath, and d. Sept. 1794.   (B.P. 1851 ed.; M.I.)

6. Dexter background black
Ermine on a chevron gules three roundles argent and in chief three crowns or (Grant), impaling, Qly or and gules a cross ermine (Camock ?)
Crest: A boar's head   Mantling: Gules and argent   Motto: Resurgam
For Henry Grant, who d. 5 July 1831. His widow d. 28 Jan. 1837. (Sources, as 2.)

NEWCASTLE EMLYN
1. Dexter background black
Qly, 1st and 4th, Gules four bars ermine three escutcheons argent (Hall), 2nd and 3rd, Gules on a chevron between three talbots' heads erased argent, collared or three bluebells proper (Hall)   In pretence: Gules on a chevron argent three cross crosslets fitchy sable (Brathwaite)
Crest: A demi-lion rampant proper holding a sword with a wavy blade proper   Mantling: Gules and argent   Motto: In coelo quies
On frame: Benjamin Edward Hall of Kilgwynn and Paddington, 1776-1849

2. All black background
On a lozenge   Arms: As 1.
On frame: Jane Maria Hall, of Kilgwynn, née Brathwaite, of Warcop Hall, 1773-1853

PENMORFA
1. Dexter background black
Qly of six, 1st, Gules a chevron ermine between three heads in profile couped proper (Lloyd), 2nd, Argent a chevron between three choughs sable each holding an ermine spot in its beak (Lloyd), 3rd, Sable a chevron between three fleurs-de-lis argent (Wynn), 4th, Vert three eagles displayed in fess or (Wynn), 5th, Or a bird sable (Corbet), 6th as 1st.
Crest: A man's head in profile couped at the shoulders proper
Mantling: Gules and ermine   Motto: Nec timet nec tumet
Unidentified

OLD RADNOR
1. Dexter background black
Argent a cross double parted sable between in the 1st and 4th quarters an eagle displayed gules and in the 2nd and 3rd quarters a lion rampant sable crowned or, the Badge of Ulster (Lewis), impaling, to dexter, Argent a lion rampant gules crowned or within a bordure engrailed sable bezanty (Cornewall), and to sinister, Argent a molet pierced sable (Ashton)
Crest: From a crown vallary a tiger statant or   Mantling: Gules and argent   Motto: Expertus fidelem
For Sir Thomas Frankland Lewis, 1st Bt., who m. 1st, 1805, Harriet, dau. of Sir George Cornewall, Bt., of Moccas, and 2nd, 1839, Mary Anne, dau. of John Ashton, and d. 22 Jan. 1855.   (Foster's Peerage, 1880 ed.)

2. Sinister background black
Qly, 1st and 4th, Argent an eagle displayed gules, 2nd and 3rd, Argent a lion rampant sable crowned or (Lewis), impaling, Argent a lion rampant gules crowned or a bordure engrailed sable bezanty (Cornewall)
Two cherubs' heads above   A large hatchment, 6 ft x 6 ft
For Harriet, 1st wife of Sir Thomas Frankland Lewis, Bt., d. 11 Aug. 1838.   (Source, as 1.)

3. Dexter background black
Two shields   Dexter, Qly, 1st and 4th, Argent an eagle displayed gules, 2nd and 3rd, Argent a lion rampant sable crowned or (Lewis), the Badge of Ulster, impaling, Qly, 1st and 4th, Argent on a cross gules five escallops or (Villiers) with crescent for difference in 1st quarter. 2nd and 3rd, Sable a chevron between three lozenges or on a canton gules a lion rampant between three cross crosslets or (Hyde), Sinister, Qly, as impalement, borne on the breast of an Imperial Eagle, each wing charged with a trefoil slipped or, and over the shield monogram with crown above. The eagle has a mace in dexter claw and orb in sinister claw

Crest: On a cap gules and ermine a tyger passant or   Motto: Expertus fidelem
For Sir George Cornewall Lewis, 2nd Bt., who m. 1844, Lady Maria Villiers, sister of William, 4th Earl of Clarendon, and d. 13 Apr. 1863.   (Foster's Peerage 1880 ed.)

RUABON

1. All black background

On a lozenge surmounted by three cherubs' heads
Qly, 1st and 4th, Argent a lion rampant azure charged on the shoulder with a fleur-de-lis or (Youde), 2nd, Argent a cross floretty between four birds sable (Edwards), 3rd, Vert a stag tippant argent armed and ungled or (Jones)   In pretence: Qly of ten, 1st, Argent a lion rampant sable (Lloyd of Plas Madoc), 2nd, Per bend sinister ermine and sable ermined argent a lion rampant or within a bordure sable bezanty (Tudor Trevor ?), 3rd, Gules a chevron between three spearheads or (   ), 4th, Argent a lion rampant sable (   ), 5th, Goutty de sang a lion rampant sable. (   ), 6th, Sable a lion rampant or (   ), 7th, Or a lion rampant sable, 8th, Vert three eagles displayed in fess or (Owen Gwynedd), 9th, Azure a lion rampant per fess or and argent a bordure argent (Karadoc), 10th, Or a lion rampant gules (Rowlands)
Motto: In pace beata quiescat   Skull in base
For Sarah, only child of Jenkin Lloyd, who m. the Rev. Thomas Youde, and d. 20 Dec. 1837, aged 92.   (M.I.)

ST DONAT'S

1. Dexter background black

Qly, 1st and 4th, Gules three chevrons argent (Iestyn Ap Gwrgant) 2nd and 3rd, Sable a chevron between three fleurs-de-lis argent (Enion ap Collwyn), impaling, Per pale azure and gules three lions rampant argent (Herbert)
Crest: A Paschal lamb   Motto: Y ddioddefws u orfu
For Morgan Stuart Williams of Aberpergwn, who m. Josephine Herbert, dau. of William Herbert of Clytha House, Monmouthshire, who d. 13 Dec. 1909   (B.L.G. 1937 ed.; M.I.)

ST GEORGE

1. All black background

Gules two lions passant in pale and in chief a rose argent (Hughes)   In pretence: Gules a chevron between three lions rampant or (Lewis)
Crest: From a ducal coronet or a demi-lion argent holding a rose argent slipped vert   Mantling: Gules and argent   Motto: Heb dduw heb ddim ddw a digon   Winged skull below
Inscribed on frame: Edward Hughes of Kinmel, b. 1738, d. 1815.
For the Rev. Edward Hughes, of Kinmel Park, who m. Mary, dau. of the Rev. Robert Lewis, and d. 1815.   (B.E.P.; inscr. on hatchment)

2. All black background

Qly, 1st and 4th, Gules two lions passant in pale between three roses in pale argent (Hughes), 2nd and 3rd, Lewis, impaling, Barry of six argent and azure, on a bend gules three bezants (Grey)
Baroness's coronet   Supporters: Dexter, A savage girt with a scimitar and holding a pike proper   Sinister, A dragon vert the wing lined or, charged with a rose argent
Inscribed on frame: Charlotte Margaret, 1st wife of 1st Baron Dinorben, born 1785, died 1835.
For Charlotte Margaret, dau. of Ralph William Grey, of Backworth, Northumberland, who m. 1804, William Lewis Hughes (cr. Baron Dinorben, 1831), as his 1st wife, and d. 21 Jan. 1835.   (Sources, as 1.)

3. All black background

Qly, as 2., impaling two coats per fess, in chief, Grey, and in base, Argent on a bend azure between two unicorns' heads erased azure three mascles or (Smyth)
Baron's coronet   Crest: As 1.   Motto: Rhad duw a rhyddid
Supporters: As 2.   On a mantle gules and ermine   Winged skull in base
Inscribed on frame: William Lewis Hughes, 1st Baron Dinorben, b. 1767, d. 1852.
For William, 1st Baron Dinorben, who m. 1st, Charlotte Margaret, dau. of Ralph William Grey, and 2nd, 1840, Gertrude, dau. of Grice Smyth, of Ballynatray, co. Waterford, and d. 10 Feb. 1852.   (Sources, as 1.)
(There is another hatchment for Baron Dinorben at Llanwenllwyfo)

4. All black background

Qly of nine, 1st, Hughes as 1., 2nd, Lewis, 3rd and 6th, Argent a chevron between three ravens sable (   ), 4th, Vert three eagles displayed in fess or (Owen Gwynedd), 5th, Gules three lions passant in pale argent (Griffith ap Cynan), 7th, Gules a chevron ermine between three stags' heads cabossed ermine (   ), 8th, Gules a lion rampant argent (   ), 9th, Argent on a bend sable three leopards' faces argent (   )
Baron's coronet   Crest and motto: As 1.   Supporters: As 2.   On a mantle gules and ermine   Winged skull in base
Inscribed on frame: William Lewis Hughes, 2nd Baron Dinorben, b. 1821, d. 1852.
For William, 2nd Baron Dinorben, who d. unm. 6 Oct. 1852.   (Sources, as 1.)

5. All black background

Qly, 1st and 4th, Hughes as 1., 2nd and 3rd, Lewis, impaling, Argent fretty gules, on a chief gules three leopards' faces or (Liddell)
No helm, but rose argent slipped vert, surmounted by a cherub's head above shield   Mantling: Gules and argent

Inscribed on frame: Florentia Emily, wife of H. R. Hughes, of Kinmel, b. 1828, d. 1909.
For Florentia Emily, 2nd dau. of Henry, 1st Earl of Ravensworth, who m. Hugh Robert Hughes, of Kinmel Park, and d. 5 Dec. 1909.   (B.P. 1965 ed.)

6. All black background
Qly, 1st and 4th, Hughes as 1., 2nd, Gules three lions passant in pale argent (Griffith ap Cynan), 3rd, Or a lion passant guardant gules (   ), impaling, Liddell
Crest, mantling and motto: As 1.
Inscribed on frame: Hugh Robert Hughes of Kinmel, born 1827, died 1911.
For Hugh Robert Hughes, of Kinmel Park, who d. 29 Apr. 1911.   (B.P. 1965 ed.)

STACKPOLE

1. Dexter background black
Qly, 1st, Or a stag's head cabossed sable attired gules (Calder), 2nd, Gyronny of eight or and sable (Campbell), 3rd, Argent a lymphad sable (Lorn), 4th, Per fess azure and gules a cross or (Lort), impaling, Qly, 1st and 4th, Barry of ten or and sable (Thynne), 2nd and 3rd, Argent a lion rampant tail knowed gules (Boteville)
Earl's Coronet   Crest: A swan wings adorsed proper crowned or
Motto: Be mindful   Supporters: Dexter, a lion guardant gules
Sinister, A hart proper
For John Frederick, 2nd Baron and 1st Earl of Cawdor, who m. Elizabeth, dau. of Thomas, 2nd Marquis of Bath, and d. 7 Nov. 1860.   (G.E.C.)

2. Sinister background black
Qly as 1., impaling, Sable three stag's heads cabossed argent attired or (Cavendish)
Countess's Coronet   Crest, Motto and Supporters: As 1.
For Sarah Mary, dau. of Gen. the Hon. Henry Compton Cavendish, who m. John Frederick Vaughan, 2nd Earl of Cawdor, and d. 21 Apr. 1881. (G.E.C.)

TALGARTH

1. All black background
Sable a fess or between two swords argent hilts and pommels or that in chief point upwards that in base point downwards (Gwynne)
Crest: A hand cuffed sable and or holding a sword argent hilt and pommel or thrust through a boar's head couped close sable langued gules tusked or   Mantling: Or and sable   Motto: Vim vi repellere licet
Unidentified

TREMEIRCHION

1. Dexter background black
Gules a lion rampant argent ducally crowned or between three crescents or (Salusbury), impaling, Azure a chevron between three hanks of cotton argent (Cotton)
Crest: A demi-lion rampant argent crowned or holding a crescent or
Mantling: Gules and argent   Motto: In coelo quies   Skull in base
For John Salusbury, of Bachegraig, who m. Hester Maria, dau. of Sir Robert Cotton, Bt., of Combermere, and d. 1762.   (B.P. 1841 ed.)

2. Sinister background black
Gules a lion rampant argent between three crescents or a canton ermine (Salusbury), impaling, Argent a chevron sable between three buckets sable banded or, each with a handle or (Pemberton)
No helm or crest, but cherub's head   Motto: In coelo quies   Winged skull in base
For Harriet Maria, dau. of Edward Pemberton, of Ryton Grove, Salop, who m. Sir John Salusbury Piozzi Salusbury, and d. 16 Apr. 1831. (B.L.G. 1871 ed.)

WELSHPOOL Museum

The original location of each hatchment as recorded by the Museum is noted in parenthesis at the end of each entry.

1. Sinister background black
Qly, 1st and 6th, Vert three eagles displayed in fess or (Wynn), 2nd, Argent two foxes counter-salient in saltire gules (Williams), 3rd, Gules three lions passant guardant in pale argent (Gruffyd ap Cynan), 4th, Sable three boys' heads couped at the neck proper their necks encircled with snakes sable (Vaughan), 5th, Sable a chevron between three fleurs-de-lis argent (   ), on the 1st quarter the Badge of Ulster   In pretence: Qly, 1st and 4th, Vert a chevron ermine between three wolves' heads argent (Vaughan), 2nd and 3rd, Sable a goat statant argent horned and hoofed or (Vaughan)
Crest: An eagle displayed or   Mantling: Gules and argent   Motto: Mors mihi lucrum
For Anne, dau. and co-heir of Edward Vaughan, of Llwydiarth, Mont., and Llangedwin, Denbigh, who m. Sir Watkin Williams-Wynn, 3rd Bt., as his 1st wife, and d.   (B.P. 1965 ed.) (Llanfihangle-yng-Ngwynfa)

2. Dexter background black
Qly, 1st and 4th, Wynn, 2nd and 3rd, Williams, on 1st quarter the Badge of Ulster   In pretence: Vert a chevron ermine between three wolves' heads erased argent (Vaughan) Also impaling, Argent a chevron between three molehills vert (Shakerley)

Wales and Monmouthshire

Crest and mantling: As 1.   Motto: Non sibi sed patriae
For Sir Watkin Williams-Wynn, who m. 1st, Anne, dau. and co-heir of Edward Vaughan, and 2nd, 1741, Frances (d. 19 Apr. 1803), dau. of George Shakerley, of Gwersyllt, Denbigh, and d. 26 Sept. 1749.   (B.P. 1965 ed.) (Llanfihangel-yng-Ngwynfa)

3. Dexter background black

Two circular shields   Dexter, Qly of six, 1st, Wynn, 2nd, Williams, 3rd, Per fess sable and argent a lion rampant counterchanged (Kyffin), 4th, Gules a chevron argent between three boars' heads or (Thelwell), 5th, Azure a cross formy fitchy argent (Cadwallader), 6th, Gules three lions passant in pale or (Gryffyd ap Cynan), in centre chief the Badge of Ulster Sinister, Qly, 1st and 4th, Wynn, 2nd and 3rd, Williams
No crest, but eagle displayed or appears behind the shield filling in the whole background   Motto: Eryr eryod eryri
For Sir Watkin Williams-Wynn, 6th Bt., who m. 1852, his cousin, Mary Emily, dau. of Rt. Hon. Sir Henry Watkin Williams-Wynn, G.C.H., K.C.B., and d. 9 May 1885.   (B.P. 1965 ed.) (Llanfihangel-yng-Ngwynfa)
(There is a duplicate hatchment at Llangedwyn)

4. Dexter background black

Qly of eighteen, 1st and 18th, Per pale azure and gules a double-headed eagle displayed or (Mytton), 2nd, Per pale sable and argent crusilly sable a double-headed eagle displayed a bordure engrailed or (   ), 3rd, Argent three tilting spears palewise in fess sable (   ), 4th, Sable three towers triple-towered argent (   ), 5th, Azure three serprents palewise in fess argent (   ), 6th, Azure a chevron argent between three fleurs-de-lis ermine (   ), 7th, Or a lion rampant gules a bordure engrailed sable (   ), 8th, Gules a lion rampant a bordure engrailed or (   ), 9th, Or a raven sable (   ), 10th, Gules a fess between six pears or (   ), 11th, Qly per fess indented gules and or, in the 1st quarter a lion passant guardant argent (   ), 12th, Sable three nags' heads erased argent (Wynn), 13th, Gules a griffin segreant or (   ), 14th, Sable a chevron or between three owls argent (   ), 15th, Gules three serpents interlaced in triangle argent (   ), 16th, Azure a chevron or between three cockerels argent (Glynne), 17th, Gules a lion rampant argent (Glynne), impaling, Qly, 1st and 4th, Sable three lions passant between four bendlets argent (Browne), 2nd, Vert a lion rampant or between three molets argent (   ), 3rd, Vert ten molets, four, three, two and one argent (   )
Crest: A demi-double-headed eagle displayed per pale or and azure
Mantling: Gules and argent   Motto: Vertu Domine sur les astres
For John Mytton, of Penylan, who m. 2nd, Beatrice Catherine, dau. of the Rev. B. Browne, vicar of Myford, and d.   (B.L.G. 5th ed.) (Meifod)

5. Sinister background black

Qly of twenty-eight, 1st to 16th, as 4., 17th, Azure three cockerels argent (Glynne), 18th, Gules a lion rampant argent (Glynne), 19th, Sable three nags' heads erased argent (Wynn), 20th, Per pale gules and or two lions rampant addorsed counterchanged (   ), 21st, Argent three greyhounds courant sable collared gules (   ), 22nd, Gules a lion rampant reguardant or (   ), 23rd, Or a lion rampant azure (   ), 24th as 21st, 25th, Argent a lion rampant sable between three fleurs-de-lis gules (   ), 26th, Argent a lion passant sable between three fleurs-de-lis gules (   ), 27th, Vert a chevron between three wolves' heads erased argent (   ), 28th, as 1st, impaling, Qly, 1st, Gules on a bend argent a lion passant sable (Davies), 2nd, Sable a chevron between three goats' heads erased or (   ), 3rd, Argent a lion passant sable a bordure engrailed gules (Llewelyn Voelgrwn), 4th, Azure three lions rampant or on a chief argent three cross crosslets sable (Mathews)

For Charlotte, only dau. of John Davies, of Marrington, Salop, who m. John Glynne Mytton, and d. 28 Sept. 1836.   (B.L.G. 5th ed.) (Meifod)

6. All black background

Qly, 1st, Per pale azure and gules a double-headed eagle displayed a bordure engrailed or (Mytton), 2nd, Sable three nags' heads erased argent (Wynn), 3rd, Azure a chevron or between three cocks argent (Glynne), 4th, Per bend sinister ermine and sable ermined argent a lion rampant or, a bordure gules (   ), impaling, Qly, 1st, Gules on a bend argent a lion passant sable (Davies), 2nd, Sable a chevron between three goats' heads erased or (   ), 3rd, Argent a lion passant sable a bordure indented gules (   ), 4th, Azure three lions rampant or on a chief argent three cross crosslets sable (   )

Crests: Dexter, A demi-double-headed eagle displayed per pale or and azure   Sinister, A cock argent armed and wattled gules   Mantling: Gules and argent   Motto: Vertu Domine sur les astres

For John Glynne Mytton, who d. Jan. 1844.   (B.L.G. 5th ed.) (Meifod)

7. All black background

Per pale azure and gules three lions rampant argent (Herbert)
Earl's coronet   Crest: A wyvern vert, in its mouth a hand couped gules   Motto: Ung je serviray   Supporters: Dexter, An elephant proper   Sinister, A griffin wings expanded argent ducally gorged gules and charged with five molets sable

Probably for Edward James, 3rd Earl of Powis, who d. unm. 7 May 1891. (B.P. 1939 ed.)

(There are similar hatchments at Llanidloes and at Cardiff Welsh Folk Museum)

8. Dexter background black

Sable three nags' heads erased argent (Lloyd), impaling, Argent on a fess engrailed plain cotised sable between in chief two molets and in base a cross

Wales and Monmouthshire

crosslet gules three bezants (Poore ?)
Crest: A horse's head argent   Mantling: Gules and argent   Motto: Nec subito nec serio
Possibly for Thomas Lloyd of Trawscoed, who m. Elizabeth Poore, and d. 1821.   (Per Museum) (Guilsfield)

9. Dexter background black
Qly, 1st and 4th, Azure a griffin segreant or (Read), 2nd and 3rd, Azure a lion rampant argent (Crewe), impaling, Qly, 1st, Gules a dexter arm in armour issuing from the sinister, holding in the hand a banner, Or on a cross between sixteen escutcheons gules a lion passant guardant or (Lake Augmentation), 2nd, Sable a bend between six cross crosslets argent (Lake), 3rd, Argent chevron between three boars' heads couped sable (Wardell), 4th, Qly argent and sable, on a bend sable three fleurs-de-lis argent (Bibye)
Crests: Dexter, An eagle displayed sable   Sinister, From a ducal coronet or a lion's gamb argent charged with a crescent azure   Mantling: Gules and argent   Motto: Sola virtute salutem   Cherub's head at each corner of shield and winged skull in base
For John Offley Crewe-Read, of Llandinam Hall, who m. 1818, Charlotte Prestwood, dau. of Sir Willoughby Lake, K.C.B., and d. 1858.   (B.L.G. 5th ed.) (Llandinam)

10. All black background
Qly, 1st and 4th, Read, 2nd and 3rd, Crewe
Crest: An eagle displayed sable   Mantling and motto: As 9.
Cherub's head at each corner of shield, and winged skull in base
Probably for Bagot Offley Crewe-Read, of Llandinam Hall, who d.s.p. Dec. 1862.   (B.L.G. 5th ed.) (Llandinam)

11. Dexter background black
Argent a lion passant guardant sable crowned or between three fleurs-de-lis gules (Pugh)   In pretence: Qly, 1st and 4th, Gules a lion rampant reguardant or (Lloyd), 2nd and 3rd, Or three boars' heads couped sable (Elystann Glodrydd)
Crest: A lion, as in the arms, holding a fleur-de-lis gules   Mantling: Gules and argent   Motto: Qui invidet minor est
Probably for David Pugh, High Sheriff of Montgomery, 1785, who m. Margaret, dau. of William Lloyd, of Montgomery, and d.s.p. 9 Feb. 1807. (B.L.G. 5th ed.) (Welshpool)

12. Dexter background black
Argent a lion passant sable between three fleurs-de-lis gules (Pryce), impaling, Argent three swans heads and necks erased sable beaked or (for Bransby)
Crest: A demi-lion sable holding a fleur-de-lis gules   Mantling: Gules and argent   Motto: Mors janua vitæ   Skull in base
For John Pryce of Gunley, who m. Mary Bransby and d.   (B.L.G. 1853 ed.) (Welshpool)

13. Dexter background black
Qly, 1st and 4th, Sable a lion rampant within an orle of cinquefoils argent, in dexter chief of 1st quarter the Badge of Ulster (Clifton), 2nd and 3rd, Argent a chevron gules between three bluebottle flowers gules slipped and leaved vert (Juckes), impaling two coats per fess, in chief, Azure a tilting-spear in pale argent, a pennon gules attached to the head and flowing to the sinister, over all a fess or (de Lancy), and in base, Per chevron sable and argent in chief three leopards' faces or (Swinfen)
Crests: Dexter, From a ducal coronet or a demi-peacock per pale sable and argent the wings expanded counterchanged   Sinister, An arm embowed in armour proper holding a tilting spear erect argent thereto affixed the Holy Standard of the Trinity, Per fess argent and sable the Device of the Trinity or, fringed gold, the ends of the streamer forked and floating behind the spear to the dexter   Mantling: Gules and ermine
Motto: Tenez le droit
For Sir Juckes Granville Clifton, 8th Bt., who m. 1st, 1794, Margaret, dau. of James de Lancy, of Bath, and 2nd, 1812, Marianne, dau. of John Swinfen, of Swinfen, Staffordshire, and d. 1 Oct. 1852.   (B.P. 1875 ed.) (Guilsfield)

14. All black background
Argent a lion rampant gules between three pheons sable (Edgerton)
Crest: Three arrows one in pale and two in saltire proper   Mantling: Gules and argent
For the Rev. Juckes Egerton, who d. 1772.   (per Museum) (Guilsfield)

WORTHENBURY

1. Dexter background black
Qly of twelve, 1st, Sable three molets argent (Puleston), 2nd, Chequy argent and sable (Warren), 3rd, Argent two lions passant guardant azure armed gules (Hanmer), 4th, Azure three boars passant in pale argent langued gules (   ), 5th, Sable three bulls' heads cabossed argent (Bulkeley), 6th, Paly of six or and gules (   ), 7th, as 3rd with label of three points gules (Hanmer), 8th, Vert a lion rampant or (Lewis), 9th, Paly of six argent and sable over all three bars gules (   ), 10th, Barry of six or and azure over all a bend gules (   ), 11th, Argent three lions passant in pale sable langued and armed gules (   ), 12th, Argent a chevron sable between three ermine tails (   ), in fess point the Badge of Ulster   To dexter of main shield, Puleston, impaling, Azure a chevron ermine between in chief two bucks salient armed and langued gules and in base a lion passant argent (Boats) S.B1.   To sinister of main shield, Puleston with Badge of Ulster, impaling, Or two ravens in pale proper (Corbet)
Crests: Dexter, On a mount vert an oak tree proper suspended therefrom an escutcheon gules charged with the Badge of the Prince of Wales   Sinister, On a chapeau gules and ermine a buck statant proper

Mantling: Gules and argent   Motto: Clariores a tenebris
For Sir Richard Price, b. 1765, assumed 1812 the surname of Puleston, created a baronet 1813, m. 1st, Ellen, dau. of William Boats, and 2nd, Emma Elizabeth, dau. of John Corbet, of Sundorne, and d. 19 May 1840. (B.P. 1875 ed.)
(There is a duplicate hatchment at Shocklach, Cheshire)

2. All black background
On an asymmetrical lozenge surmounted by an urn
Puleston, with Badge of Ulster, impaling Corbet
Cherub's head to dexter, sinister and in base
For Emma Elizabeth, widow of Sir Richard Puleston, Bt., who d. Jan. 1850, aged 73.   (B.P. 1875 ed.)

3. Sinister background black
Qly of twelve, as 1., but with following differences, 6th, Paly of six or and sable, 8th, Sable a lion rampant or, Badge of Ulster in chief on impalement line, impaling, two coats per fess, in chief, Argent two bars wavy gules (England), and in base, Sable three lozenges ermine a bordure gules (Shaw)
Three cherubs' heads above and winged skull below
For Eliza Shaw, of Chester, who m. 1816, as his 2nd wife, Sir Richard Puleston, 2nd Bt. (his 1st wife, Annette, dau. of Lt.-Gen. England, d. Oct. 1814), and d. 17 Nov. 1847.   (B.P. 1875 ed.)

WREXHAM, Plas Power
1. Dexter background black
Ermine two flaunches sable on a chief gules four martlets or (FitzHugh), impaling, Sable a chevron between three pelicans' heads erased or vulning themselves proper (Godfrey)
Crest: A martlet proper legs and beak gules   Mantling: Gules, or and argent   Motto: In moderation is my glory
For Thomas FitzHugh, who m. 1814, Philadelphia Elizabeth, dau. of Peter Godrey, of Old Hall, Suffolk, and d. 1856, aged 86.   (B.L.G. 1871 ed.)
(The current whereabouts of this hatchment is unknown)

BETTWS
1. All black background
Argent on a fess sable three stags' heads erased or (Bradford)
Crest: A stag's head erased or   Mantle: Gules and argent
For Richard Bradford, who was buried 17 April 1816, aged 68.   (M.I.)

APPENDIX 1:
Hatchment locations by County

Location	Old County	New County
Bettws	Glamorgan	Mid Glamorgan
Capel Llanilterne	Glamorgan	Mid Glamorgan
Cardiff	Glamorgan	South Glamorgan
Clyro	Radnor	Powys
Denbigh	Denbigh	Clwyd
Erddig	Denbigh	Clwyd
Gresford	Denbigh	Clwyd
Haverfordwest	Pembroke	Dyfed
Kerry	Montgomery	Powys
Llanafan	Cardigan	Dyfed
Llanbedrog	Caernarvon	Gwynedd
Llanbethian	Glamorgan	South Glamorgan
Llandudno	Caernarvon	Gwynedd
Llandybie	Caernarvon	Gwynedd
Llandyfriog	Cardigan	Dyfed
Llandyrnog	Denbigh	Clwyd
Llanelltyd	Merioneth	Gwynedd
Llanfair-ar-y-brun	Carmarthen	Dyfed
Llanfor	Merioneth	Gwynedd
Llangedwyn	Denbigh	Clwyd
Llangian	Caernarvon	Gwynedd
Llangoedmor	Cardigan	Dyfed
Llangollen	Denbigh	Clwyd
Llanidloes	Montgomery	Powys
Llannanno	Radnor	Powys
Llannon	Carmarthen	Dyfed
Llarnrhaidr-ym-Mochnant	Denbigh	Clwyd
Llansantffraid Glyn Ceirog	Denbigh	Clwyd
Llanstephan	Carmarthen	Dyfed
Llantwit Major	Glamorgan	South Glamorgan
Llanwenllwyfo	Anglesey	Gwynedd
Llanynys	Denbigh	Clwyd
Machynlleth	Montgomery	Powys
Margam Abbey	Glamorgan	West Glamorgan
Montgomery	Montgomerty	Powys
Myddfai	Carmarthen	Dyfed
Nanteos, Aberystwyth	Cardigan	Dyfed
Neath	Glamorgan	West Glamorgan
Newcastle Emlyn	Carmarthen	Dyfed
Penmorfa	Caernarvon	Gwynedd
Old Radnor	Radnor	Powys
Ruabon	Denbigh	Clwyd
St Donat's	Glamorgan	South Glamorgan
St George	Denbigh	Clwyd
Stackpole	Pembroke	Dyfed
Talgarth	Brecknock	Powys
Tremeirchion	Flints	Clwyd
Welshpool	Montgomery	Powys
Worthenbury	Flints	Clwyd
Wrexham	Denbigh	Clwyd

SCOTLAND

Blair Athol 2: For James Robertson, 1803
(*Photograph by courtesy of Mr. C. J. Burnett*)

INTRODUCTION

The trading and political links between the Low Countries and Scotland, from the medieval period until the creation of the United Kingdom, influenced many facets of life in England's northern neighbour. The unique characteristics of Scotland are an amalgam of continental and native practices which have led to national traditions, particularly in the use of heraldry. The control and utilisation of armoury are quite different from those in England.

Funeral hatchments in Scotland are not the same as in England. They follow the north European tradition. Instead of the simple achievement of Arms, there are additional elements surrounding the deceased's armorial ensigns, pinned to a broad black border. These elements consist of small shields, cut-out tears, mortheads (often accompanied by crossed bones), and ciphers. These indicated both familial relationships and healthy emotion at the loss of a loved one. The small shields illustrate paternal descent on the dexter side and maternal descent on the sinister. The aim was to show eight armigerous ancestors on both sides to demonstrate the seize quartiers of true nobility. Such a combination of emotional feeling and pride in blood is typical of the difference in national characteristics between the inhabitants of Scotland and England.

Sadly few hatchments remain in their original condition with all these elements present. One can be found furth of Scotland in the Netherlands at Medemblick Kirke. This commemorates Lord George Murray, son of the first Duke of Atholl, who died in exile during 1760 as a result of being the commanding General of the Jacobite army in 1745/46. All the elements are painted on a piece of canvas without the extra border of black material. There are 16 probative shields, four mortheads, his cipher L.G.M. for Lord George Murray, and a central full achievement of Arms. The remaining area of black background is covered with white tears. A restored hatchment of 1803 at Blair Atholl (No. 1) retains probative shields, mortheads and ciphers. Following the Union of the Parliaments in 1707 Scotland experienced the new phenomenon of English influence which affected hatchment practice. The earliest surviving example dates from 1758 (Haddington, Lenoxlove Castle) and shows the background coding system of England with a residual winged morthead below the Arms. However, old customs did not entirely disappear and a hatchment created six years later in 1764 (Edinburgh, Royal Museum of Scotland, No. 3) orignally had the wide black border bearing the usual additions. Even as late as 1833 the traditional Scottish hatchment was still in use at Murthly Castle, Perthshire (No. 3).

A revival of the Scottish hatchment style is found in the work of Graham Johnstone (1869-1927) who created hatchments in 1896, 1903, and 1910 having borders bearing tears, ciphers and symbols of death. He softened the earlier honest attitude by substitution of sentimental winged angels heads or laurel-wreathed torches for the mortheads and bones. By doing so he reflected the altered attitude to the perception of death at the end of Queen Victoria's reign.

Apart from Graham Johnstone, who painted five hatchments, the only other known artist was H. W. Lonsdale, who was based in London. He executed heraldic work for John, third Marquess of Bute, including the illustrations for two books on Scottish burgh heraldry co-authored by Bute. Lonsdale produced preparatory designs for Bute's hatchment and may also have been responsible for its execution. It is now in the private chapel at Mount Stewart, Rothesay. Between the date of the earliest extant hatchment, 1758, and Graham's first hatchment of 1896, there were 13 holders of the appointment Herald Painter to the Court of the Lord Lyon. So far insufficient research has been undertaken on personal painting style to attribute hatchments to specific painters. More is known about funerary painting undertaken by Herald Painters during the 16th and 17th century, but none of their work is extant except for a Roll, which illustrates how the heraldic elements should be marshalled in a funeral procession.

Two identical funeral hatchments were painted. There exists a painter's account of 1666 confirming this practice which shows that one hatchment was erected above the main door of the deceased's residence and the second was placed in the church of interment. Extant duplicates can be found at Cavers and Hawick for Lady Theresa Eliott of Stobs (died 1836) and at Murthly Castle for Sir William Drummond Stewart of Grandtully who died in 1871. The Eliott of Stobs hatchments were employed again in 1864 following the death of Lady Theresa's husband, by the simple expedient of blacking out the dexter white background.

The heraldic author, George Seton, gives three examples of the use of hatchments in Edinburgh during the 19th century: that of the Countess of Wemyss hung outside the family town house at 64 Queen Street in 1850; the hatchment of Adam Urquhart which was displayed in his house in St Colme Street after his death in 1860; and lastly the hatchment of Prince Albert of Saxe-Coburg and Gotha, Consort of Queen Victoria, surmounting the entrance to the Palace of Holyrood House in 1861. Another hatchment to the Prince was also exhibited above the porte-chochère at Balmoral Castle. The most recent hatchment display in Scotland's capital took place in 1988 at Arthur Lodge following the death of John Pinkerton QC.

Because of the additional border, hatchments are larger in Scotland, several being almost two metres square. This caused problems in smaller churches. At Wem Old Kirk in Perthshire there remains a hatchment frame which is hinged to allow access through the narrow entrance doorway. Most hatchments are painted on canvas, but there are two exceptions. At Hunterston Castle a wooden panel has been used, and at Preston Parish Kirk the hatchment is painted on a sheet of tin. The latter was originally positioned inside the subterranean vault of the Grant-Sutties of Balgone and the painter may have considered tin would provide a more permanent memorial than canvas!

There are 53 known hatchments in Scotland but others may exist in family vaults now permanently closed. Like so many surviving heraldic artefacts they provide evidence of customs no longer in general use. They also help to give identity to the unique practice of armoury in Scotland.

C. J. BURNETT
3 Hermitage Terrace, Edinburgh

ALYTH, Perthshire
1. Dexter background black
Two oval shields   Dexter, Argent an eagle displayed sable, beaked and membered gules (Ramsay),   Sinister, Qly, 1st, Azure three cinquefoils argent (Fraser), 2nd, Argent a lion rampant gules surmounted of a bend sable (Abernethy), 3rd, Gules three lioncels argent (Ross), 4th, Argent three piles in chief gules (Wishart)
Crest: Unicorn's head couped argent maned and horned or   Motto: Spernit pericula virtus   Supporters: Two griffins proper   All on a mantle gules and ermine and suspended between the shields the badge of a Baronet of Nova Scotia
For Sir George Ramsay, of Banff, 6th Bt., who m. Eleanora, dau. of George, 14th Lord Saltoun, and d. 16 Apr. 1790, following a duel.
(G.E.C. Bt.)

BLAIR ATHOLL
Kilmaveonaig Episcopal Church, Perthshire
1. Sinister background black
Gules a dexter hand couped proper fesswise holding a cross crosslet fitchy in pale sable between three wolves' heads erased argent (Robertson of Lude), impaling, Qly, 1st and 4th, Or on a fess between in chief three crosses formy gules and in base a mullet azure three bezants (Mercer of Aldie), 2nd, Per pale sable and argent a chaplet of four groups of three leaves counterchanged (Nairne), 3rd, Azure three mullets argent within a double tressure flory counter-flory or (Murray)
Motto: Resurgam   A cherub's head above the shield   A morthead and crossbones at base
For Margaret, dau. of the Hon. Robert Nairne and his wife Jean Mercer, heiress of Aldie, who m. James Robertson, of Lude, and d. 1802.
(B.L.G. 1853 ed.)

2. All black background
Robertson of Lude, with cross crosslet fitchy azure, impaling, Qly, 1st and 4th, Or on a fess between three mullets gules three annulets argent, (for Mercer of Aldie), 2nd, Per pale sable and argent a chaplet azure (Nairne), 3rd, Murray
Crest: A sleeping dog proper   Mantle: Gules and ermine   Mottoes: (above crest) Dinna waken sleeping dogs   (Below shield) Ductus non coactus   Supporters: Two horses rampant argent
The hatchment is surrounded by a black felt border on which are fixed

mortheads and crossbones in the top and bottom angles, and the initials JR and ESQ in the dexter and sinister angles respectively. On this border are fixed the probative branches as follows;

Top to bottom

Dexter	*Sinister*
Gardyn	Lathom
Gordon of Abergeldie	Earl of Exeter
Graham of Inchbrackie	Earl of Tullibardine
Cambell of Clenorchy	Earl of Derby
Farquharson of Invercauld	Marquess of Atholl
Lord Murray	Lord Nairne
Unframed	

For James Robertson of Lude, who d. 1803.   (Sourches, as 1)

CAVERS, Roxburghshire
1. All black background, originally sinister background black
Two shields   Dexter, surrounded by the motto of a Baronet of Nova Scotia with badge pendant below, Qly, 1st and 4th, Gules on a bend or a baton sable tipped or, on a chief azure a castle between two columns all proper inscribed with gold letters PLUS ULTRA (Eliott with Augmentation of Gibralter), 2nd and 3rd, Gules on a bend engrailed or a baton azure within a bordure or charged with eight roundels azure (Eliott), Sinister, as dexter, impaling, Qly, 1st and 4th, Argent three-masted ship at anchor within a double tressure flory counter-flory or (Boswell of Auchinleck), 2nd, Argent three bars sable (Auchinleck of that Ilk), 3rd, qly i. & iv. Argent a lion rampant azure (Bruce, Earl of Kincardine), ii. & iii. Argent a saltire and a chief gules (Bruce)
Supporters: Dexter, A ram,   Sinister, A goat, each gorged with a laurel wreath and each with their interior foot resting upon a battlement on a rock proper   A winged cherub's head in top angle
For Theresa, dau. of Sir Alexander Boswell Bt., who m. Sir William Francis Eliott Bt. of Stobs, and d. 1836, and subsequently used for her husband who d. 3 Sept. 1864.   (B.P. 1875 ed.)

CROMARTY East Church, Ross & Cromarty
1. All black background
Gules a mullet between three lions rampant argent (Ross)
Crest: A demi-lion rampant argent   Mantling: Gules and argent
Motto: Virtus repulsæ nescia
Possibly for Duncan Munro Ross of Cromarty who d. unm. 14 Jan 1887. (B.L.G. 1937 ed.)

DUNBLANE Cathedral Museum, Perthshire
1. All black background
On a lozenge   Argent on a fess between in chief two annulets and in

base two crosiers in saltire sable three mullets pierced argent within a bordure gules (Fogo)
For Jane Mathie, dau of David Fogo of Row and wife of Rev. John Laurie, who assumed the name Fogo. She died 10 June 1889.
(C.J.B.)

2. All black background
Arms as 1
Crest: A cross crosslet fitchy gules   Mantling: Gules and argent
Surrounded by a blank border, semé de larmes, top and bottom angles a winged cherub's head, dexter and sinister angles a torch with sprig of laurel
Motto: Fuimus
For David Fogo Laurie Row-Fogo who d. Oct. 1903.   (C.J.B.)
Unframed and signed by Graham Johnstone

DURIE LEVEN, Fife
1. All black background
Or a saltire between in chief a demi-lion dismembered, in base a cross formy gules and in the flanks two mullets sable (Christie)
Crest: A dexter hand holding a missive letter proper   Mantling: Gules and argent   Motto: (above crest) Pro Rege
The initials R and C are at the left and right angles and the border, decorated by four mortheads and crossbones, is semé de larmes
For Robert Christie of Durie who d. 29 Aug. 1896.   (B.L.G. 1937 ed.)
Painted by Graham Johnston

EDINBURGH, Arthur Lodge
1. All black background
Or a chevron vert between in chief a dexter hand couped at the wrist grasping a dagger point uppermost flanked by two cross crosslets fitchy and in base a lymphad, sail furled, oars in action, flagged azure all gules
Crest: A demi wild cat rampant guardant gules   Mantling: Vert and or
Motto above: Be kind
For John MacPherson Pinkerton, Q.C., who d. 27 Sept. 1988
Painted by J. W. Howells.   (C.J.B.)

EDINBURGH, Formerly at St Margaret's Convent
1. All black background
Per fess or and azure a galley proper sail furled and flagged gules, in dexter chief a hand couped fessways holding a cross crosslet fitchy gules and in sinister chief a cross crosslet fitchy gules all within a bordure argent (Assumed arms of James Gillis)   Behind the shield are in saltire an Archbishop's staff and crossier   Above the shield is a mitre surmounted by an Archbishop's hat from which hang green cords with ten

tassels on either side of the shield
Motto: Scio qui servio   On the reverse of the hatchment are the initials: I.G/R.I.P.
For James Gillis, titular bishop of Limyra and coadjutor vicar apostolic Eastern District of Scotland, who d. July 1864.   (Catholic Directory)

EDINBURGH, Royal Museum of Scotland
1. Dexter background black
Argent a fess wreathed azure and gules (Carmichael), impaling, Gules three antique crowns or, on a canton argent a demi-otter issuing out of a bar wavy sable, all within a bordure ermine (Grant)
Crest: A dexter hand and arm in armour holding a broken spear proper
Mantling: Gules and argent   Motto: Toujours Prest   Supporters: Dexter, A chevalier in complete armour, plumed on the head with three feathers argent holding in his right hand a baton royal,   Sinister, A horse argent furnished gules
For John, 4th Earl of Hyndford, who m. Janet, dau. of William Grant, Lord Prestongrange, and d. 21 Dec. 1787.   (G.E.C.)

2. All black background
On a lozenge   Grant, impaling, Argent a cross moline quartered pierced argent within a bordure chequy azure and argent ? (Millar)
For Grizel, widow of William Grant d. 1792.   (B.P.)

3. Dexter background black
indecepherable and a bordure ermine (for Grant), impaling, A cross square-pierced within a bordure chequy (for Millar)
Mantling: Gules and argent   Crest, motto and supporters:Indistinguishable   This hatchment is in very poor condition and the charges and tinctures are barely distinguishable
For William Grant, Lord Prestongrange, who m. Grizel Millar and d. 1764. (Source, as 2)
(This hatchment, together with Nos 1. and 2. are unframed and were formerly in the Prestongrange Burial Vault, Preston Parish Church, East Lothian)

FRAZERBURGH, St Peter's Episcopal Church, Aberdeenshire
1. All black background
Two oval shields   Dexter, within the circlet of the Order of the Thistle, Qly, 1st and 4th, Azure three cinquefoils argent (Fraser), 2nd, Or a lion rampant gules surmounted of a bend sable (Abernethy), 3rd, Argent three piles gules (Wishart)   Sinister, Qly as dexter, impaling, Qly, 1st, Argent on a chevron cotised sable three portcullises with rings and chains argent (Thurlow), 2nd and 3rd, Sable a cross or (Hovell), 4th, Or on a chief indented sable a crescent argent (   )   Below the shields are the Badges of the Orders of the Thistle, Maria Theresa of Austria, Bath, Hanoverian Guelphic Order and St George of Russia

Baron's coronet   Crest: An ostrich proper holding a horseshoe in its beak   Mantle: Gules and ermine   Motto: In God is all
Supporters: Two angels with wings expanded and endorsed proper and vested in long garments or
For Alexander, 16th Lord Saltoun, K.T., G.C.B., G.C.H., who m. Catherine, natural dau. of Edward, 1st Baron Thurlow, Lord Chancellor, and d. 18 Aug. 1853.   (G.E.C.)

GIFFORD, Yester Church, East Lothian

1. Sinister background black

Within the collar and badge of the Order of the Thistle and the ribbon and badge of the Order of the Bath, Qly, 1st and 4th, Azure three cinquefoils argent (Fraser), 2nd and 3rd, Gules three bars ermine (Gifford), on an inescutcheon, Argent three escutcheons gules (Hay), and impaling, Qly, 1st and 4th, Argent three lozenges conjoined in fess gules within a bordure sable (Montagu), 2nd and 3rd, Or an eagle displayed vert beaked and membered gules (Monthermer)
Marquess's coronet   Crest: A goat's head erased argent armed or   Mantling: Gules and ermine   Motto: Spare nought   Supporters: Two bucks proper attired and ungled or each gorged with a collar azure charged with three cinquefoils argent
For Susan, dau. of William, 5th Duke of Manchester, who m. George, 8th Marquess of Tweedale, K.T., G.C.B., and d. 5 Mar. 1870.   (G.E.C.)

HADDINGTON, Lennoxlove Castle, East Lothian

1. Dexter background black

Two oval shields   Dexter, within the circlet of the Order of the Thistle, Qly, 1st and 4th, qly i. & iv. Gules three cinquefoils ermine (Hamilton), ii. & iii. Argent a lymphad sable (Arran), 2nd and 3rd, Argent a heart gules imperially crowned or, on a chief azure three mullets argent (Douglas)   Sinister, Gules on a fess between three doves argent as many crosses formy gules (Gunning)
Duke's coronet   Crest: Out of a crest coronet an oak tree fructed and penetrated transversely in the mainstem by a frame saw proper inscribed: Through   Mantling: Gules and ermine   Motto: Through
Supporters: Two antelopes argent ducally gorged chained and armed or
Pendant beneath the dexter shield is the reverse of the Badge of the Order of the Thistle. At base of hatchment is a winged morthead
For James, 6th Duke of Hamilton, 3rd Duke of Brandon, K.T., who m. Elizabeth, dau. of John Gunning, of Castle Coote, and d. 17 Jan. 1758.
(B.P. 1841 ed.)

2. Dexter background black

Two oval shields   Dexter, within the Order of the Garter with Great George pendant below, Qly, 1st and 4th, qly, i. & iv. Hamilton, ii. & iii. Arran, 2nd and 3rd, qly, i. Azure a lion rampant argent crowned or (Macdowell), ii. Or a lion rampant gules surmounted of a ribbon sable

(Abernethy), iii. Argent three piles gules, (Wishart), iv. Or a fess chequy argent and azure surmounted on a bend gules charged with three buckles or (Stewart of Bonkill), In pretence (on 2nd and 3rd grand quarters), Argent a human heart gules crowned or and on a chief azure three mullets argent (Douglas), Overall an escutcheon ducally crowned, Azure three fleurs-de-lis or (Dukedom of Chatelherault)   Sinister, Qly as dexter, impaling, Qly, 1st and 4th, Per pale gules and azure on a chevron argent between three martlets or an eagle displayed sable within on a bordure or a double tressure flory counter-flory gules (Beckford), 2nd and 3rd, qly i. & iv. Hamilton, ii. & iii. Arran
Duke's coronet   Crests: Dexter, as 1.   Sinister, on a chapeau gules turned up ermine a salamander in flames proper for Douglas   Mottoes: Above sinister crest, Jamais arriere   Below, Through   Supporters: As 1.
For Alexander, 10th Duke of Hamilton and 7th Duke of Brandon, K.G., who m. Susan Euphemia, dau. and co-heir of William Beckford of Fonthill Abbey, who d. 18 Aug. 1852.   (G.E.C.)

3. Dexter background black
Qly as dexter of 1 with Arran as 2.   In pretence: surmounted by the Grand Ducal crown of Baden, Or a bend gules (Grand Duchy of Baden)
Duke's coronet   Crests: As 2.   Mantle: Gules and ermine
Mottoes: As 2.   Supporters: Dexter, As 1.   Sinister, A griffin regardant crowned or
For William, 11th Duke of Hamilton and 8th Duke of Brandon, who m. Princess Mary, dau. of Charles Louis Frederick, Grand Duke of Baden and d. 15 July 1863.   (G.E.C.)

HAWICK, Wilton Lodge Museum, Roxburghshire
1. All black background (originally sinister background black)
Two shields   Dexter, surrounded by the motto of a Baronet of Nova Scotia with badge pendant below, Qly, 1st and 4th, Gules on a bend or a baton sable tipped or, on a chief azure a castle between two columns all proper inscribed with gold letters: Plus Ultra (Eliott with Augmentation of Gibralter), 2nd and 3rd, Gules on a bend engrailed or a baton azure within a bordure or charged with eight bezants (Eliott), Sinister, as dexter, impaling, Qly, 1st and 4th, Argent on a fess sable three cinquefoils argent, on a canton azure a three-masted ship at anchor within a double tressure flory counter-flory or (Boswell of Auchinleck), 2nd, Argent three bars sable (Auchinleck of that Ilk), 3rd, qly i. & iv. Argent a lion rampant azure (Bruce, Earl of Kincardine), ii. & iii. Argent a saltire and a chief gules (Bruce)
Supporters: Dexter, A ram,   Sinister, A goat, each gorged with a laurel wreath and each with their interior foot resting upon a battlement on a rock proper   A winged cherub's head in top angle
For Theresa, dau. of Sir Alexander Boswell, Bt., who m. Sir William Francis Eliott, Bt., of Stobs, and d. 1836, and subsequently used for her

Scotland

husband who d. 3 Sept. 1864. (B.P. 1875 ed.)
Indentical to Cavers No 1.
(Stamped on the reverse: Prepared by Robertson and Miller, 51 Long Acre, London, R & M 1779)

HUNTERSTON Castle, Ayrshire

1. All black background

Vert three greyhounds courant argent collared or, on a chief argent three hunting horns vert, garnished gules (Hunter of Restennet).
Crest: A greyhound sejant proper collared or   Mantling: Gules and argent   Motto: Cursum perficio   The shield is flanked on either side by a winged angel's head
Unidentified

INNERPEFFRAY Chapel, Perthshire

1. All black background

Qly, 1st and 4th, Or three bars wavy gules (Drummond), 2nd and 3rd, Or a lion's head erased within a double tressure flory counter-flory gules (Drummond Augmentation)
Crests: Dexter, A goshawk jessed and belled proper,   Sinister, The eagle of St John with the nimbus held in the beak   Mottoes: (above shield) Prius mori quam fidem fallere   (below shield) Virtutem coronat honos   Supporters: Two savages wreathed about the temples and loins with oak leaves and holding in the exterior hands clubs over the shoulder all proper
For Andrew John Drummond, de jure 7th Viscount Strathallan, who d. unm. 20 Jan. 1822.   (G.E.C.)

2. All black background

On a lozenge surmounted by a Baroness's coronet
Drummond, impaling, Argent a chevron sable between three boars' heads erased gules, langued azure, (Elphinstone)
On a mantle gules and ermine   Supporters: As 1., but standing on a mount vert semé of caltraps
For Clementina, dau. of Charles, 10th Lord Elphinstone, who m. James Drummond, Baron Drummond of Stobhall (d. 2 July 1800), and d. 31 Aug. 1822.   (G.E.C.)
(These two hatchments were restored in 1974 at the Stenhouse Conservation Centre)

INVERCAULD Castle, Aberdeenshire

1. All black background (originally dexter background black)

Qly, 1st and 4th, Or a lion rampant gules, 2nd and 3rd, Argent a fir tree growing out of a mount, on a chief gules the Royal Banner of Scotland and on a canton argent a hand issuing from the sinister side, holding a dagger point downwards proper (Farquharson of Invercauld), impaling,

Argent a lion rampant gules within a bordure engrailed ermine (Dundas of
Arniston)
Crest: A demi-lion rampant gules holding a sword in its dexter paw
proper, pommelled or   Mantling: Gules and argent   Motto: Fide et
fortitudine   Supporters: Two wild cats rampant guardant
For James Farquharson, 12th of Invercauld, who m. Janet, dau. of Gen.
Francis Dundas, and d. 22 Nov. 1862, and also used for his wife who
d. 2 Aug. 1869.   (B.L.G. 1937 ed.)

LADYKIRK Church, Berwickshire
1. Dexter background black
Gules three wolves' heads erased within a bordure argent (Robertson)
In pretence: Robertson, with a wild man in chains lying fesswise under
both the shield and the escutcheon
Baron's Coronet   Crest: A right arm holding an imperial crown
Mantle: Gules and ermine   Mottoes: (above crest) Virtutis gloria
merces   (below shield) Advance with courage   Supporters: Two bay
horses proper, stirrups, saddle and bridle argent chained or, pendant
therefrom a shield of arms, Argent on a chief gules a cushion between
two mullets argent pierced of the field (Majoribanks)
For David Majoribanks, who assumed the name Robertson by Royal
Licence in 1834, who m. Marrianne Sarah, dau. and co-heiress of Sir
Thomas Haggerstone, Bt., by Margaret, only dau. and heiress of William
Robertson, of Ladykirk. He was created Baron Majoribanks of Ladykirk
on 12 June 1873, and d. 19 June 1873.   (G.E.C.)

LADYKIRK House, Berwickshire
1. All white background (originally dexter background black)
Qly, 1st and 4th, Sable a fess or between three asses passant argent,
maned and unguled or (Askew), 2nd, Qly or and gules in the first quarter
a blackbird proper (Craster), 3rd, Argent on a chevron engrailed between
three martlets azure three crescents or (Watson)
Crest: A dexter hand holding on a poignard erect proper, hilt and pommel
or, a saracen's head couped and embrued proper, wreathed about the
temples with a torse argent and gules tied with ribands of the same
Mantling: Sable, gules and argent   Mottoes: (over crest) Fac et spera
(below shield) Patientia casus exuperat omnes
Probably for George Adam Askew, of Pallinsburn, who m. his cousin
Anne Elizabeth Askew, and d.s.p. 1838.   (B.L.G. 1937 ed.)
Unframed

LUSS, Dunbartonshire
1. Dexter background black
Argent a saltire engrailed sable (Colquhoun), impaling, Gules three
mullets or (Sutherland)
Crest: A hart's head couped gules   Mantling: Gules and argent
Mottoes: (above) Si je puis,   (below) Cnoc elachan   Supporters: Two
ratchounds proper collared sable   A winged morthead below the shield

Scotland 123

The letters Sr. J C Bt. in the four angles
For Sir James Colquhoun, 1st Bt., who m. Helen, dau. of William, Lord
Strathnaver, and d. 16 Nov. 1786.   (G.E.C. Bt.)

2. All black background
On a lozenge   Arms: As 1.
Crest: A hart's head erased gules   Mantling: Gules and argent
Motto: Si je puis   Supporters: As 1.   The letters L H S in left,
right and bottom angles
For Helen, widow of Sir James Colquhoun, d. 7 Jan. 1791.   (Source, as 1.)
Unframed

3. Dexter background black
Colquhoun with Badge of Ulster in centre chief, impaling, Qly 1st, Azure a
ship at anchor within a tressure flory counter-flory or, 2nd and 3rd, Or a
lion rampant gules, 4th, Azure a ship under sail or, over all and dividing
the quarters a cross engrailed sable and all within a bordure quarterly or
and gules charged with three mullets or (Sinclair of Ulbster)
Crest, mantling, mottoes and supporters: As 1.
For Sir James Colquhoun, 3rd Bt., of Luss, who m. Janet, dau. of Sir John
Sinclair, Bt., of Ulbster, and d. 3 Feb. 1836.   (Source, as 1.)

4. All black background
On a lozenge   Colquhoun, impaling, Gules in chief on a crest wreath
argent and sable an eagle's head couped proper in base on a crest wreath
argent and sable a boar's head erased proper
Crest, mantling, motto and supporters: As 2.   The letters J C in bottom angle
Possibly for Jane, dau. of Sir Robert Abercromby, of Birkenbog, who m.
Sir James Colquhoun, 4th Bt., and d. 3 May 1844.   (Source, as 1.)

5. All black background
On a lozenge   Arms: As 3.   Supporters: As 1.
For Janet, Widow of Sir James Colquhoun, 3rd Bt., who d. 21 Oct. 1846.
(Source, as 1.)

6. Background a mantle gules and ermine
Colquhoun with Badge of Ulster
Crest, mottoes and supporters: As 1.
Possibly for Sir James Colquhoun, 4th Bt., who was drowned in Loch
Lomond, 18 Dec. 1873.   (Source, as 1.)

7. Dexter background black
Colquhoun with Badge of Ulster, impaling, Argent a fess azure between in
chief two mullets and in base a lion rampant gules (MacRae of Conchra)
Crest: A hart's head couped gules attired or   Mantling: Gules and argent
Motto: (behind crest) Si je puis   Supporters: Two Ratchounds argent
collared sable   At base of hatchment are the initials AJC flanked by the
dates 1838 and 1910. The canvas is surrounded by a black border, semé de

larmes, in the dexter and sinister angles of the frame are the monograms AJC and AHM respectively, in top and bottom angles are a winged cherubs head. For Sir Alan John Colquhoun, 6th Bt., of Luss, who m. 2nd, Anna Helena, dau. of Duncan MacRae, of Conchra, who d. 1910.   (B.P.)
(This hatchment was painted by Graham Johnstone)

MURTHLY Castle, Perthshire

1. All black background

Qly, 1st, Or a fess chequy argent and azure (Stewart), 2nd, Sable a stag's head cabossed proper (Mackenzie), 3rd, Gules three human legs armed flexed and conjoined at the thigh (Isle of Man), 4th, Argent a lymphad sails furled and oars in action sable (Lorne), all within a bordure azure charged with eight buckles or (Stewart of Grandtully)
Crests: Dexter, Two bees counter volant proper   Sinister, The sun in splendour or   Motto: (above shield) Provide   (in base) Respicit aeque
Supporters: Dexter, A man armed cap a pied proper holding lance palewise
Sinister, A horse rampant argent
Suspended beneath the shield from a ribbon which is tied in a true lovers knot above the shield, is an incorrectly painted Badge of a Baronet of Nova Scotia
Possibly for an unm. dau. of Sir John Stewart, 4th Bt., of Grandtully

2. Dexter background black

Qly, as 1, but, Azure a stag's head cabossed or, for Mackenzie, impaling, Or three bars wavy gules (for Drummond of Logie Almond)
Crests: As 1.   Mottoes: (above crests) Provide   (in base) Respicit aeque
Supporters: Dexter, A man armed cap a pied proper holding a spear palewise
Sinister, A horse rampant argent
Suspended beneath the shield is the Badge of a Baronet of Nova Scotia
The hatchment is surrounded by a black felt border to which are pinned a winged cherub's head in the top angle, a morthead and crossbones on the dexter and sinister angles and the following probative shields:-

Top to bottom

Dexter	Sinister
Stewart of Grandtully Bt.	Mercer of Aldie Kt.
Hon. Sir James Mackenzie of Royston Bt.	Dow of Arnhall
Earl of Cromartie	Mercer of Aldie Bt.
Mackenzie of Rosehaugh	Lindsay of Evelick Bt.
Missing	Sibbald of Rankeilor Bt.
Sinclair of Mey Bt.	
Stewart of Ballechin	

For Sir George Stewart of Grandtully, 5th Bt., who m. Catherine, dau. of John Drummond, of Logie Almond, and d. 9 Dec. 1827.   (G.E.C. Bt.)

3. All black background

Qly, 1st and 4th, Stewart, 2nd and 3rd, Lorne, all within a bordure azure charged with seven buckles or (Stewart of Grandtully),   In pretence: Or three bars within a bordure all wavy gules, (Drummond of Logie Almond)
Crest: Two bees counter volant proper   Mantling: Gules and argent   Motto:

Provide   The shield is encircled by a ribbon from which is suspended a
Badge of a Baronet of Nova Scotia
On a surrounding black border, semé de larmes, a winged cherub's head in chief
with morthead and crossed bones in the dexter and sinister angles
For Catherine, widow of Sir George Stewart, who d. 1833.   (Source, as 2.)

4. Dexter background black
Qly, 1st and 4th, Stewart of Grandtully, as 3, 2nd, qly, i. Mackenzie as 2, ii.
Or a burning mount proper (Macleod), iii. Isle of Man, iv. Argent a pale sable,
(for Erskine ?) 3rd, qly, i. & iv. Drummond as 2, ii. Stewart, iii. Lorne,
impaling, Qly, 1st and 4th, Or a lion rampant within a double tressure flory
counter-flory gules within a bordure compony argent and azure (Stuart), 2nd,
Or a fess chequy argent and azure (Stuart), 3rd, Or three cushions two and
one within a double tressure flory counter-flory (Randolf, Earl of Moray)
Crest: As 3.   Mantling: Gules and argent   Motto: Provyd
Supporters: As 2.   The badge of a Baronet of Nova Scotia is suspended
below the shield   The surrounding black border has lost any additions.
For Sir John Archibald Stewart, 6th Bt., who m. Lady Jane Stuart, dau. of
Francis, 9th Earl of Moray, and d. May 1838   (Source, as 2.)

5. All black background
On a oval shield placed upon the Cross of the Sovereign and Military Order
of Malta
Qly, 1st and 4th, Or a fess chequy argent and azure between in chief three
buckles azure and in base a galley sable oars in action flagged gules (Stewart),
2nd, qly, i. Gules an imperial crown within a double tressure flory counter-
flory or, ii. Azure a stag's head cabossed or, iii. Argent a pale sable, iv. Isle of
Man, (Cromartie), 3rd, Drummond as 2.
For Thomas Stewart, 4th son of George, 5th Bt., of Grandtully, Knight of
the Sovereign Order of Malta, who d. 18 July 1846.   (B.P. 1875 ed.)

6. All black background
Qly, 1st and 4th, Stewart as 5, 2nd, Drummond as 3., 3rd, qly, i. Or a
mountain in flames proper, ii. Azure a stag's head cabossed or, iii. Gules three
human legs armed proper, fixed, conjoined at the thighs or, iv. Argent on a
pale sable an imperial crown proper within a double tressure flory counter-
flory, all within a bordure ermine (Second matriculation of Stewart of
Grandtully 1839)
Crest, mantling, and motto as 4.   Supporters: As 1.   Badge of a
Baronet of Nova Scotia pendant below shield
For Sir William Drummond Stewart, of Grandtully, 7th Bt., d. 28 Apr. 1871.
(Source, as 5.)

7. Identical to 6

PERTH St John's Kirk
1. All black background
Or on a fess gules between in chief three crosses formy gules and in base a
mullet azure, three bezants (Mercer of Aldie)

Crest: A stork's head couped holding a serpent proper   Mottoes: (above) The grit poui   (below) Crux Christi nostra corona   Supporters: Two wild men helmeted and holding clubs proper   All on a mantle gules and ermine   Skull in base
Possibly for Lawrence James Mercer, who d. unm. 20 Aug. 1791. (B.L.G. 1853 ed.)

PRESTONPANS, East Lothian
1. Sinister background black
Qly, 1st and 4th, i. & iv. Barry wavy of six azure and or on a chief or a lion rampant naissant double queued vert (Suttie), ii. & iii. Argent a chevron chequy gules and argent between three hunting-horns sable garnished gules within a bordure gules (Semple), 2nd and 3rd, Gules three ancient crowns or on a canton argent a demi-otter issuing out of a bar wavy sable (Grant of Pretongrange), impaling, Qly, 1st and 4th, qly i. & iv. Or a lion rampant gules armed and langued azure (Wemyss), ii. & iii. Argent a fess azure within a double tressure flory counter-flory gules (Charteris of Amisfield), 2nd & 3rd, qly i. & iv. quarterly, first and fourth, Argent a heart gules crowned on a chief azure three mullets argent (Douglas), second and third, Azure a bend between six cross crosslets fitchy or on a bordure or a double tressure flory counter-flory gules, ii. & iii. Gules a lion rampant argent, on a bordure argent eight roses gules (Earldom of March),
Crests: Dexter, A ship under full sail proper,   Sinister, A man's head affronté couped below the shoulders   Mantling: Gules and ermine
Motto: (above dexter crest) Nothing hazard nothing have   (above sinister crest) Non interiora secutus   Pendant below the shield the Badge of a Baronet of Nova Scotia
For Harriet, dau. of Francis, 8th Earl of Wemyss, who m. Sir George Grant-Suttie, Bt., of Balgone, and d. 30 May 1858. (B.P. 1875 ed.)

ROSSLYN Chapel, Midlothian
1. All black background
Qly of eight, 1st, 4th and 8th, Argent a cross engrailed sable (St Clair), 2nd, Argent a pale sable (Erskine), 3rd, Azure a bend between six cross crosslets fitchy or (Mar), 5th and 6th obliterated by black paint, 7th, Argent a chevron between three roses gules (Wedderburn)
Earl's Coronet surmounting a Knight's Helm   Crest: A demi-phoenix in flames proper   Mantling: Gules and ermine   Mottoes: (above crest) Illaeso lumine solem   (below shield) Fight   Supporters: Dexter, An eagle surgeant-tergiant proper   Sinister, A griffin wings elevated proper
Possibly for James Alexander George St Clair-Erskine, styled Lord Loughborough, eldest son of the 3rd Earl Rosslyn, who d.v.p. 28 Dec. 1851; or for James, 2nd Earl of Rosslyn, who m. Henrietta, dau. of the Hon. Edward Bouverie. She died 8 Aug. 1810, and he died 18 Jan. 1837. (G.E.C.)

ROTHESAY Mount Stuart, Isle of Bute
1. All black background
On a lozenge   Qly, 1st, Argent a fess chequy azure and argent within a double tressure flory counter-flory gules (Stuart), 2nd, Argent a lion rampant

Scotland

azure (Crichton), 3rd, Gules a saltire argent between twelve cross crosslets or (Windsor), 4th, Per pale azure and gules three lions rampant argent (Herbert), In pretence: Azure a lion rampant argent (for North), impaling, Qly, 1st, Argent a maunch sable (Hastings), 2nd, Argent a fess between three pheons sable (Rawdon), 3rd, Gyronny of eight ermine and gules, (Campbell of Loudoun), 4th, Per pale or and argent on a fess azure three mullets argent, (Mure) Marchioness's coronet   Mantle: Gules and ermine
For Sophia, dau. of Francis, 1st Marquess of Hastings, m. as the 2nd wife of John, Marquess of Bute, and d. 28 Oct/Dec. 1859. The Marquess had m. as his 1st wife, Maria, dau. of George, 3rd Earl of Guildford   (G.E.C.)

2. All black background
On a lozenge with many tinctures very faded
Qly, as dexter of 1, with escutcheon of pretence, Azure a lion passant or between three fleurs-de-lis argent (North), impaling, Qly, 1st, blank, 2nd, a fess sable, 3rd, Campbell, 4th, Per fess faded and azure in base a mullet
Coronet and mantle: As 1.
For Sophia, Lady Bute: As 1.

3. Dexter background black
Two shields   Dexter, within the circlet of the Order of the Thistle with Badge pendant below, Qly, 1st and 4th, Stuart as 1 with field or, 2nd and 3rd, Crichton   Sinister, within ornamental wreath, Qly as dexter, impaling, Qly, 1st, Gules on a bend between six cross crosslets argent the Augmentation of Flodden and a crescent for difference (Howard of Glossop), 2nd, Gules three lions passant guardant in pale or a label of three points argent (Brotherton), 3rd, Chequy or and azure (Warren), 4th, Gules a lion rampant or (Fitzalan)
Marquess's coronet   Crests: A demi-lion rampant gules, with motto above Nobilis est ira leonis   A wyvern proper holding in its mouth a sinister hand couped gules   A wyvern, fire issuant from its mouth all proper
Supporters: Dexter, A horse argent bridled gules   Sinister, A stag attired or
Motto: Avito viret honore
For John Patrick, 3rd Marquess of Bute, K.T., who m. Gwendolen Mary Anne, dau. of Edward, 1st Baron Howard, of Glossop, and d. 9 Oct. 1900.   (G.E.C.)

WEEM Old Church, Perthshire
1. All black background
Argent a chief gules (Menzies)
Crest: A man's head bearded proper wreathed vert   Mantling: Gules and argent   Mottoes: (above crest) Will God I shall   (below) Resurgam
Supporters: Two wild men wreathed about the temples and hips and bearing clubs, all proper   Suspended below the shield is the badge of a Baronet of Nova Scotia   Morthead in base. Black surround has lost any additions
Possibly for Sir John Menzies of that Ilk, 4th Bt., who d. 1800.   (B.P. 1875 ed.)

2. All black background
Identical to No. 1

3. Dexter background black

Menzies, impaling, Azure a maunch ermine overall a bend gules (Norton)
Crest: A bearded man proper couped at the shoulders and wreathed about the temples   Mantling: Gules and argent   Motto: Will God I shall   Supporters: As 1.   Pendant below the shield is the badge of a Baronet of Nova Scotia   A broad dark blue velvet border, devoid of additions, surrounds the hatchment.
Stamped on the back: I Mundell, Edinburgh. Prepared by Charles Robertson, 51 Long Acre, London, C.R.1827.
For Sir Neil Menzies of that Ilk, 6th Bt., who m. 2nd, Grace Conyers Charlotte, sister of Fletcher, 3rd Baron Grantley, and d. 20 Aug. 1844.
(Source, as 1.)

4. All black background

On a lozenge   Menzies arms only
Motto and Supporters as 2.   Suspended below the shield is the Badge of a Baronet of Nova Scotia the ribbon of which is tied in a lover's knot above the shield   The frame covered in velvet is decorated with two mortheads and crossbones in dexter and sinister angles and fourteen paper tears
Possibly for Caroline Elizabeth Wynford, dau. of 6th Bt., and d. 17 Feb. 1845.
(Source, as 1.)

5. All black background

Menzies arms only
Suspended below the badge of a Baronet of Nova Scotia
Crest: As 1.   Mantling: Gules and argent   Motto: Vil God I zal
Supporters: Two wild men wreathed about the loins and temples with laurel
For Sir Neil James Menzies of that Ilk, 8th and last Bt., who d.s.p. 21 Dec. 1910.   (B.P.)
(Painted by Graham Johnstone)

6. A badly damaged, unidentified fragment for a member of the Menzies family

7. Frame with fragment of canvas painted by Graham Johnstone

Unknown Location

All black background

Qly, 1st and 4th, Or three crescents within a double tressure flory counter-flory gules (Seton), 2nd and 3rd, Argent three escutcheons gules (Hay of Tillbody)   Behind the shield, in saltire, two spears bearing on their points a Royal Helmet and a shield bearing the Royal Arms of Scotland, as the Badge of the Office of Heritable Royal Armour Bearer
Crest: A boar's head couped or langued gules   Motto: Forward ours
Supporters: Two greyhounds proper
Possibly for Archibald Seton, of Touch, Royal Armour Bearer, who d. before 1835.

INDEX

Abercromby, Jane, 123
Acton, Susanna, 25
Adams, Clare, 54
Alcock, 40
Archer, Harriet, 19
Ashton, Mary Anne, 98
Askew, Anne Elizabeth, 122
Askew, George Adam, 122
Astley, Sir John (2nd Bt.), 64
Atcherley, David Francis, 48
Atcherley, Richard, 48

Baden, Princess Mary of, 120
Bagot, Mary, 56
Ball, Capt. Henry, 74
Banner, Frances, 19
Barneby, Mary, 14
Barneby, William, 14
Basnett, Rev. John, 31
Baugh, Harriet, 39
Baugh, Isabella, 12
Beale, Anne, 38
Beckford, Susan Euphemia, 119
Bell, Sarah Frances, 10
Bennet, Mary, 36
Benthall, Richard, 31
Berwick, Richard, 4th Baron, 29
Berwick, Richard, 5th Baron, 29
Berwick, William, 6th Baron, 29
Birt, Jane, 77
Blayney, Arthur, 48
Blount, John, 7
Boats, Ellen, 106
Bolas, Roger, 46
Bond, Catherine, 81
Boscawen, George, 81
Boswell, Theresa, 116, 120
Botfield, Thomas, 43
Bough, Anne, 11
Bourne, 86

Bradford, Richard, 107
Bradshaw, 8
Bransby, Mary, 105
Brathwaite, Jane Maria, 97, 98
Bridgeman, Judith, 60
Bridgeman, Lucy Elizabeth, 51
Browne, 31
Browne, Beatrice, 103
Brydges, 17
Brydges, Ann, 18
Brydges, Francis William Thomas, 17
Brydges, William, 17
Bullen, 73
Bunbury, Annabella, 81
Burnaby, Laura Gertrude, 83
Burton, Edward, 45
Burton, Rev. Henry, 27
Burton, Robert, 27, 28
Burt, Louisa, 75
Bushby, Mary, 74
Bute, John Patrick, 3rd Marquess of, 126, 127
Butler, Lady Charlotte, 95
Butler, Mary, 80
Butt, Charlotte, 35

Caldecott, Elizabeth, 84
Calder, John (1st Earl of Cawdor), 101
Calder, John (2nd Earl of Cawdor), 101
Card, Jane, 17
Carmichael, John (4th Earl of Hyndford), 118
Carne, Elizabeth, 93
Carne, Rev. Robert, 93
Cavendish, Sarah Mary, 101
Cawdor, John, 1st Earl of, 101
Cawdor, John, 2nd Earl of, 101
Chambre, Catherine, 46

Champneys, Sir Thomas Swymmers Mostyn, Kt., 86, 87
Childe, Elizabeth, 9
Christie, Robert, 117
Clarke, 18
Clarke, Jane, 18
Clavering, 58
Clifton, Sir Jukes Granville (8th Bt.), 106
Clive, Rev. Archer, 20
Clive, Edward Bolton, 19
Clive, Edward, (1st Earl of Powis), 47
Clive, Sir Edward, Kt., 19
Clive, George, 19
Clive, Judith, 19
Clough, Rev. Thomas, 81
Clowes, 65
Cludde, Edward, 68
Cludde, Mary, 68
Cockburne, Lucretia, 55
Cock, Rachel, 97
Colchester, Jane, 74, 75
Colquhoun, Sir James (1st Bt.), 122, 123
Colquhoun, Sir James (3rd Bt.), 123
Colquhoun, Sir James (4th Bt.), 123
Colquhoun, Sir Alan John (6th Bt.), 123
Congreve, 58
Congreve, John, 58
Cooper, Lissey Anne, 33
Coppinger, Marian, 8
Corbet, 60, 61, 62
Corbet, Sir Andrew Vincent (2nd Bt.), 62
Corbet, Sir Andrew, Kt., 61
Corbet, Elizabeth, 62
Corbet, Emma Elizabeth, 106, 107
Corbet, John, 31
Corbet, Capt. Richard, 60
Corbet, Richard Prynce, 65
Corbet, Sir Vincent, Kt., 60
Corbett, Ellen, 45
Corbett, Rev. Joseph, 45
Corbett, Panton, 45
Corbett, Sir Richard (4th Bt.), 44
Corbett, Robert, 45
Cornewall, Rt. Rev. Folliat Herbert, 39
Cornewall, Frederick, 39
Cornewall, Harriet, 98
Cornewall, Herbert, 39
Cornish, Susannah, 30
Cotes, John, 51
Cotes, Rev. Washington, 62
Cotton, Hester Maria, 102
Crawford, Margaret Alice, 87
Crawley, Jane Elizabeth, 67
Crewe-Read, Bagot Offley, 105
Crewe-Read, John Offley, 105
Curre, William, 74
Curzon, Mary Catherine, 52

Dansey, Matty, 45
Davenport, Rev. Edmund Sharrington, 67
Davenport, Mary Elizabeth, 42
Davenport, William Sharrington, 67
Davenport, William Yelverton, 67
Davies, 78
Davies, Charlotte, 104
Davies, John, 35
Davies, Rt. Hon. Somerset, 19
de Lancy, Margaret, 106
Denison, Maria, 34
Digby, Frances, 7
Dinorben, William (1st Baron), 100
Dinorben, William (2nd Baron), 100
Down, Emma, 11
Drummond, Andrew John (7th Viscount Strathallan), 121
Drummond, Catherine, 124
Drummond, James (Baron), 121
Dundas, Janet, 121
Dungannon, Arthur, 2nd Viscount, 92

Eardley, 57
Edwardes, Major Benjamin, 55
Edwardes, Ellen Hester, 39
Edwardes, Sir Francis (4th Bt.), 57
Edwardes, Sir Henry (5th Bt.), 58
Edwardes, Sir Henry (9th Bt), 41
Edwardes, John Thomas Smitheman, 56
Edwards, 77
Edwards, Eleanor, 58

Index 131

Edwards, Eliza Constantia, 36
Edwards, Elizabeth, 48
Edwards, Jennet, 94
Edwards, John, 49
Edwards, Mary Cornelis, 94
Edwards, Richard, 89, 90
Edwards, William, 94
Egerton, Rev. Jukes, 106
Eliott, Sir William (7th Bt.), 116, 120
Elphinstone, Clementina, 121
England, Annette, 107
Eustace, Alicia, 38
Evans, Kingsmill, 18
Evelyn, 8
Eyton, Anne, 44

Farquharson, James, 121
Finch, Essex, 86
FitzHugh, Thomas, 107
Fitzwilliams, Charles Home, 87
Fitzroy, Charlotte, 92
Fleming, 6
Fletcher, Margaret, 26
Fogo, Jane Mathie, 116
Foley, Hon. Edward, 16
Ford, Elizabeth, 9
Forester, 29
Forester, Cecil, 34
Forester, Cecil, 1st Baron, 66
Forester, George, 66
Forester, John George, 2nd Baron, 67
Fraser, Alexander, (16th Lord Saltoun), 118
Fraser, Eleonora, 115
Fraser, George, (8th Marquess of Tweedale), 119

Gage, Charlotte Margaret, 16
Garbett, Francis, 9
Gardner, Hannah, 92, 93
Gatacre, Edward, 36, 37
Gibbons, Richard, 63
Gillis, James, 117
Gittins, Mary, 27
Glynn, Rev. Sir Stephen (7th Bt), 36
Godfrey, Philadelphia, 107
Godolphin, 44

Goodrich, Caroline Helena, 43
Gordon, Eliza, 82
Gouge, Robert Minors, 14
Gould, Sir Charles (1st Bt.), 73
Grant, Charles Robert Archibald, 51
Grant, Gen. Sir Charles John, 51
Grant, Henry, 97
Grant, Janet, 118
Grant, William, 118
Grant-Suttie, Sir George, Bt., 126
Grazebrook, Thomas Worrall, 37
Grey, Charlotte, 93, 100
Griffin, Alfred William, 50
Griffiths, Charles Griffith, 91
Griffith, Thomas, 81
Guise, Elizabeth Mary, 78
Gunning, Elizabeth, 119
Gwynne, 101
Gwynne, Anna Maria, 96
Gwynne, Sackville Henry, 88, 89

Habington, Thomas, 6
Haggerstone, Marrianne, 122
Hallifax, Rev. Robert Fitzwilliam, 13
Hall, Benjamin Edward, 97, 98
Hamilton, Alexander, 10th Duke of, 119
Hamilton, Anne, 39
Hamilton, Gustavus, (6th Viscount Boyne), 39
Hamilton, James, 6th Duke of, 119
Hamilton, William, 11th Duke of, 120
Hamond, Anne, 19
Hanbury, Elizabeth August, 35
Hancock, Anne, 15
Hanmer, Edward, 48
Harnage, Sir George (2nd Bt.), 43
Harnage, William Henry, 42
Harvey, Louisa, 27
Harwood, Abigail, 58
Harwood, John, 58
Harwood, Richard (4th Baron Berwick), 29
Harwood, Richard (5th Baron Berwick), 29
Harwood, William (6th Baron Berwick), 29
Hastings, Sophia, 126, 127

Hatton, 65
Heaton, John, 80
Heaton, Richard, 80
Herbert, Edward (3rd Earl of Powis), 77, 91, 104
Herbert, Elizabeth, 87
Herbert, George (2nd Earl of Powis), 95
Herbert, Harriet Avarina, 83
Herbert, Henrietta, 47
Herbert, John Owen, 82
Herbert, John, 82
Herbert, Josephine, 99
Heywick, 59
Hill, 49
Hill, Andrew, 49
Hill, Anna Maria, 12
Hill, Anne, 27
Hill, Sir Francis Brian, Kt., 33
Hill, Lucy, 49
Hill, Mary, 58, 97
Hill, Rachel, 62
Hill, Thomas, 28
Hodges, Thomas, 49
Hodgetts, Eliza Maria, 16
Hodgetts-Foley, John Hodgetts, 16
Holford, Col. James Price, 96
Holland, Frances, 41
Holland, Martha, 52
Holland, Margaret, 81
Homfray, Samual, 74
Hope, John Thomas, 39
Hope, Louisa Mary, 41
Hope-Edwardes, Thomas Henry, 40
Hopton, Rev John, 6
Hosier, 32
Hosier, Rebekah, 32
Hoskyns, 5
Hoskyns, Sir Hungerford (6th Bt.), 13
Hoskyns, Sir Hungerford (7th Bt.), 14
Houblon, Arabella, 41
Howard, Charles (11th Duke of Norfolk), 8
Howard, Gwendolen, 127
Hughes, Anne, 66
Hughes, Anna Maria, 10

Hughes, Rev. Edward, 99
Hughes, Gwen Gertrude, 94
Hughes, Hugh Robert, 100, 101
Hughes, William (1st Baron Dinorben), 93, 100
Hughes, William (2nd Baron Dinorben), 100
Humphreston, Frances, 60
Hunt, Roland, 30
Hunter, 121
Husbands, Mary, 19
Hyndford, John, 4th Earl of, 118

Irvine, Sophia, 53
Isted, Anne, 45

Jefferies, Elizabeth, 57
Jefferies, Harriet, 63
Jenkins, Sir Richard, Kt., 59
Jenkinson, Catherine, 50
Jenkinson, Charles (3rd Earl of Liverpool), 50, 51
Jenkinson, Louisa Harriet, 51
Jenkins, Harriet, 37
Johnson, Harriet, 82
Johnstone, 38
Jones, Elizabeth, 40, 80
Jones, Harriet, 42
Jones, Joanna, 9
Jones, Lucy Favoretta, 45
Jones-Parry, Lt-Gen Sir Love Parry, 84
Jones-Parry, Thomas Parry, 84

Kinchant, Eliza, 55
Knight, Frances, 25
Knill, Barbara, 8
Kynaston, Anne, 52
Kynaston, Corbet, 62
Kynaston, Jane, 63
Kynaston, Margaret, 52
Kynaston, William, 52, 63
Kynnersley, Thomas, 44
Lacon, Richard, 44
Lake, Charlotte, 105
Lancy, de, Margaret, 106
Lascelles, Anna, 76
Lascelles, Frances, 76

Index 133

Laurie, John, 116
Lawley, Robert (1st Baron Wenlock), 34
Lee-Warner, Rev. Daniel Henry, 18
Leighton, Sir Baldwin (6th Bt), 26
Leighton, Sir Brian (9th Bt), 26
Leighton, Sir Charlton (4th Bt), 26
Leighton, Emma Elizabeth, 31
Leighton, Francis Knivett, 54
Leighton, Rev. Francis, 54
Leighton, Louisa Charlotte, 40
Leighton, Sir Robert (5th Bt), 26
Leigh, Henry (8th Viscount Tracy), 48
Lewis, Sir George Cornewall (2nd Bt.), 98
Lewis, Mary, 99
Lewis, Sir Thomas Frankland (1st Bt.), 98
Liddell, Florentia Emily, 100, 101
Lister, Dorothy, 64
Liverpool, Charles, 3rd Earl, 50, 51
Lloyd, 81, 98
Lloyd, Alice Mary, 47
Lloyd, Annabella, 37, 89, 90
Lloyd, Charles Spencer, 44
Lloyd, Dorothea, 81
Lloyd, Gen Sir Evan, Kt., 38
Lloyd, Frances, 89
Lloyd, John Arthur, 43
Lloyd, Margaret, 90, 91, 105
Lloyd, Mary, 30
Lloyd, Sarah, 99
Lloyd, Thomas, 90, 104
Lloyd, William, 27
Lloyd, Rev. William, 27
Londonderry, George, 5th Marquess of, 94
Long, Walter, 83
Lowe, Thomas, 49
Lutley, Jenks, 40
Lyde, Margaret, 8
Lygon, Elizabeth, 9
Lyster, Jane, 32
Lyster, Richard, 25, 26

Mackworth, Sir Robert Humphrey (2nd Bt.), 97
MacRae, Anna Hellena, 123
Madocks, John, 88
Majoribanks, David, 1st Baron, 122
Maltzan, Alexandrina, 67
Manley, Ann Frances Pole, 13
Manners, Katharine Mary, 66
Marindin, Catherine, 67
Martin, Charlotte, 49
Matthews, Elenora, 91
Matthews, Frances, 92
Mears, George, 92, 93
Menzies, Caroline Elizabeth Wynford, 128
Menzies of that Ilk, Sir John, (4th Bt.), 127
Menzies of that Ilk, Sir Neil, (6th Bt.), 128
Menzies of that Ilk, Sir Neil James, (8th Bt.), 128
Mercer of Aldie, Lawrence James, 125
Mercer, Margaret, 115
Middelton, Anna Maria, 52
Miers, 96
Miers, John Nathaniel, 97
Miers, Mary Anne, 97
Miers, Nathaniel, 97
Milford, Richard, 1st Baron, 82
Millar, Grizel, 118
Milman, Gen. Francis, 76
Mitchell, Elizabeth, 83
Money-Kyrle, Elizabeth Mary, 11
Money-Kyrle, Sir James, Bt, 10
Money-Kyrle, Rev. William, 11
Monington, Bridget, 16
Montagu, Susan, 119
More, Rev. Robert, 47
More, Thomas, 47, 53
Moreton, 53
Morgan, 63
Morgan, Rev. Charles Augustus, 76
Morgan, Charles, 15
Morgan, Charles (1st Baron Tredegar), 74
Morgan, Charles, 75
Morgan, Sir Charles (2nd Bt.), 73
Morgan, Hester, 9
Morgan, Jane, 73, 74

Morgan, John, 75
Morgan, Maria Margaretta, 76
Morgan, Thomas, 74, 75
Morgan, Col. Thomas, 75
Morse, Anne, 55
Mostyn, Anna Maria, 88
Mostyn, Charlotte, 86, 87
Mostyn, Sir Roger (3rd Bt.), 86
Mostyn, Sir Thomas (4th Bt.), 86
Mostyn, Sir Thomas (6th Bt.), 86
Moultrie, Harriet, 57
Muckleston, Anne, 58
Muckleston, Edward, 57
Muckleston, Elizabeth, 30
Muckleston, Joseph, 30
Muckleston, William Hawkins, 30
Mundy, Rosamund, 74
Myddelton, Col. John, 80
Myddelton, Maria Sydney, 79
Myddelton, Lt.-Col. Ririd, 78
Myddelton, Robert, 79
Myddelton, Rev. Robert, 79
Myddelton, William, 79
Mynors-Baskerville, Thomas Baskerville, 15, 78
Mytton, 54
Mytton, Barbara, 32
Mytton, Harriet, 38, 53
Mytton, John Glynne, 104
Mytton, John, 42, 103
Mytton, Richard, 41, 42
Mytton, Thomas, 37, 47

Nairne, Lady Mary Margaret, 78, 115
Neave, Sir Arundell (4th Bt.), 94
Newton, 36
Noel, Mary, 28
Noneley, Thomas, 46
Norfolk, Charles, 11th Duke of, 8
Northwick, George, 3rd Baron, 35
North, Maria, 126
Norton, Grace Conyers, 128

Oakeley, Catherine, 28
Oakeley, Richard, 19
Oakeley, William, 47

Ogilvie, Mary, 79
Ottley, 50
Ottley, Adam, 50
Owen, Avarina Brunetta, 82
Owen, Frances Maria, 29
Owen, Harriett, 42, 55
Owen, Rev. Hugh, 63
Owen, Letitia, 42

Palk, Mary, 83
Palmer, William Henry (4th Bt.), 91
Panton, Jane Josepha, 45
Parker, Mary, 6
Parry, Margaret, 84
Parry, Mary, 14, 15, 75
Pelham, Frances, 38
Pemberton, Edward, 68
Pemberton, Harriet Maria, 102
Philips, 64, 65
Philips, Ann, 17
Philips, Richard (1st Baron Milford), 82
Philips, Sarah, 14
Piggott, Anna, 26
Pigott, Anne, 31
Pigott, Rebecca, 42
Pinkerton, John Macpherson, 117
Pippard, Mary, 44
Pole, Mary, 32
Poore, Elizabeth, 104
Powell, 96
Powis, Edward (Clive), 1st Earl of, 47
Powis, Edward (Herbert), 1st Earl of, 47, 91, 104
Powis, George (Herbert), 2nd Earl of, 95
Powys, Anne, 28, 49
Powys, Emily Lissey, 33
Powys, Henry, 64
Powys, John, 32
Powys, Thomas, 32
Powys, Thomas Henry, 33
Powys, Thomas Jelf, 33
Presland, Frances, 30
Presland, Rev. Thomas, 30
Price, Elizabeth, 7
Price, John, 77

Index

Price, Richard Watkin, 89
Price, Susanna, 90
Primrose, Lady Sybil, 51
Probyn, Alice, 83
Pryce, 66
Pryce, John, 105
Pryce, Penelope, 26
Pryce, Richard, 35, 36
Prynce, Mary, 64
Pugh, David, 105
Puleston, Sir Richard (1st Bt.), 106, 107
Puleston, Sir Richard (2nd Bt.), 107

Rainsford, Mary, 42
Ramsay, Sir George (6th Bt.), 115
Rice, Catherine, 17
Ricketts, Anne Fane, 5
Ricketts, Eliza Bourke, 13
Ricketts, Harriet Ann, 13
Robertson, David, 122
Robertson, James, 115
Roberts, Rev. Nathaniel, 92
Roberts, Sidney, 88
Rocke, Anne, 57
Rocke, Rev. John, 38
Rocke, Mary Anne, 56
Rocke, Richard, 55
Rodd, Mary, 26
Ross, Duncan Munro, 116
Row-Fogo, David Fogo Laurie, 117
Rushout, George (3rd Baron Northwick), 35
Rushout-Bowles, Rev. George, 34

St Clair-Erskine, James Alexander George, 126
St Leger, Louisa Ann, 54Saltoun, Alexander, (16th Lord), 118
Salt, Thomas, 57
Salusbury, 80
Salusbury, Sir John Salusbury Poizzi, 102
Salusbury, John, 102
Salwey, Arthur, 13
Salwey, Edward, 13
Salwey, John, 11

Salwey, Richard, 12
Salwey, Theophilus Richard, 12
Sandford, Humphrey, 40
Sandford, Rev. Humphrey, 41
Scott, George Jonathan, 33
Scott, George, 55
Scott, Rev. George, 55
Scott, Richard, 54, 55
Scudamore, 3rd Viscount, 7
Scudamore, Charles Fitzroy, 7
Scudamore, Frances, 7, 8
Scudamore, James, 7
Seton, Archibald, 128
Severne, Lt.-Gen. John, 65
Shakerley, Frances, 102
Shaw, Catherine, 79
Shaw, Eliza, 107
Shetliffe, Rev. George Thomas, 11
Shuckburgh, Julia Evelyn, 50
Simes, Sarah Antoinette, 88
Sinclair, Janet, 123
Skelhorne, Lucy, 43
Slaney, Robert Aglionby, 30
Smitheman, Catherine, 55
Smitheman, Rose, 28
Smith, Mary, 25
Smythies, Mary Anne, 88, 89
Smyth, 48
Smyth, Gertrude, 93, 100
Sneyd, Elizabeth, 27
Somerset, Charlotte, 39, 56
Spottiswoode, Elizabeth, 59
Stackhouse, John, 25
Stackhouse-Acton, Thomas Pendarves, 25
Stanford, Anne, 63
Stanhope, Catherine, 13
Stanley, Marguerita, 26
Stephens, John, 91
Stevenson, Sophia, 84
Stewart of Grandtully, 124
Stewart of Grandtully, Sir George (5th Bt.), 124
Stewart of Grandtully, Sir John Archibald (6th Bt.), 125
Stewart of Grandtully, Thomas, 125
Stewart of Grandtully, Sir William (7th Bt.), 125

Stewart, Caroline, 34
Stoney, Mary, 73
Strangways, Mary Lucy, 95
Strathallan, Andrew, 7th Viscount, 121
Stuart, Lady Jane (Moray), 125
Stuart, John Patrick, (3rd Marquess of Bute), 126, 127
Sutherland, Helen, 122, 123
Swinburne, Charlotte, 56
Swinburne, Thomas, 56

Talbot, Christopher Rice, 95
Talbot, Thomas Mansel, 95
Tayleur, 68
Tayleur, William, 58
Taylor, Anne Caroline, 10
Taylor, Mary, 61
Tey, 64
Thomas, Rice, 90, 91
Thoroton, Anne Roosilia, 18
Thurlow, Catherine, 118
Thursby, Rev. George August, 38
Thynne, Elizabeth, 101
Tongue, Elizabeth, 67
Topping, Anne Margaret, 48
Topp, Edward Lingen, 66
Topp, Jane, 66
Topp, Richard, 66
Townshend, Anne, 34
Tredegar, Charles, 1st Baron, 74
Trevor, Arthur Edwin, 1st Baron, 52
Trevor, Arthur, (2nd Viscount Dungannon), 92
Trevor, Arthur, (3rd Viscount Dungannon), 53
Tweedale, George, 8th Marquess of, 119

Vane, George, (5th Marquis of Londonderry), 94
Vaughan, Anne, 102
Vaughan, Ernest (4th Earl of Lisburne), 83
Vaughan, Ernest (5th Earl of Lisburne), 83
Vaughan, Sir Henry, 87
Vaughan, Sir Robert Williams (2nd Bt.), 88
Venables, Sarah, 80
Villiers, Lady Maria, 98

Walcott, Catherine, 28
Wall, 10
Walsham, Elizabeth, 9
Walsham, John Garbett, 10
Walsham, Sir John James (1st Bt.), 10
Walsham, John, 8, 9
Walters Robert, 91
Waring, 46
Weaver, Susannah, 48
Webb, 50
Wemyss, Harriet, 126
Wenlock, Robert, 1st Baron, 34
Western, Sarah, 86
Westfaling, Mary, 5
Whitehurst, 64
Wicksted, Richard, 65
Wigley, Caroline, 20
Wilkes, Elizabeth, 37
Williams, 6
Williams, Edward, 32
Williams, Grace Anne, 6
Williams, Morgan Stuart, 99
Williams, Richard, 32
Williams, William, 94
Williams-Wynn, Mary Emily, 89, 103
Williams-Wynn, Sir Watkin (3rd Bt.), 102
Williams-Wynn, Sir Watkin (6th Bt.), 89, 103
Wingfield, John, 56
Wingfield, Rowland, 56
Wolryche-Whitmore, William, 51
Wood, 59
Wren, Theodosia Ann Martha, 5
Wren-Hoskyns, Chandos, 5
Wynne, Augusta Frances, 33
Wynne, Catherine, 79

Yorke, Simon, 81
Youde, Rev. Thomas, 99